YORK NOTES

# Paddy Clarke Ha Ha Ha

Roddy Doyle

Note by Chrissie Wright

 Longman  York Press

Chrissie Wright is hereby identified as author of this work in accordance with Section 77 of the Copyright, Designs and Patents Act 1988

YORK PRESS
322 Old Brompton Road, London SW5 9JH

PEARSON EDUCATION LIMITED
Edinburgh Gate, Harlow,
Essex CM20 2JE, United Kingdom
Associated companies, branches and representatives throughout the world

First published 1999

ISBN 0–582–38196–7

Designed by Vicki Pacey
Illustrated by Judy Stevens
Phototypeset by Gem Graphics, Trenance, Mawgan Porth, Cornwall
Colour reproduction and film output by Spectrum Colour
Produced by Addison Wesley Longman China Limited, Hong Kong

# CONTENTS

# PREFACE

York Notes are designed to give you a broader perspective on works of literature studied at GCSE and equivalent levels. We have carried out extensive research into the needs of the modern literature student prior to publishing this new edition. Our research showed that no existing series fully met students' requirements. Rather than present a single authoritative approach, we have provided alternative viewpoints, empowering students to reach their own interpretations of the text. York Notes provide a close examination of the work and include biographical and historical background, summaries, glossaries, analyses of characters, themes, structure and language, cultural connections and literary terms.

If you look at the Contents page you will see the structure for the series. However, there's no need to read from the beginning to the end as you would with a novel, play, poem or short story. Use the Notes in the way that suits you. Our aim is to help you with your understanding of the work, not to dictate how you should learn.

York Notes are written by English teachers and examiners, with an expert knowledge of the subject. They show you how to succeed in coursework and examination assignments, guiding you through the text and offering practical advice. Questions and comments will extend, test and reinforce your knowledge. Attractive colour design and illustrations improve clarity and understanding, making these Notes easy to use and handy for quick reference.

York Notes are ideal for:
- Essay writing
- Exam preparation
- Class discussion

Chrissie Wright was educated at Durham University and the Open University and is head teacher of a school in Middlesbrough. She has many years of experience as a senior examiner for English and English Literature with one of the largest examination boards.

The text used in this Note is the 1995 Heinemann New Windmills edition.

*Health Warning:* **This study guide will enhance your understanding, but should not replace the reading of the original text and/or study in class.**

# PART ONE

# INTRODUCTION

## HOW TO STUDY A NOVEL

You have bought this book because you wanted to study a novel on your own. This may supplement classwork.

- You will need to read the novel several times. Start by reading it quickly for pleasure, then read it slowly and carefully. Further readings will generate new ideas and help you to memorise the details of the story.
- Make careful notes on themes, plot and characters of the novel. The plot will change some of the characters. Who changes?
- The novel may not present events chronologically. Does the novel you are reading begin at the beginning of the story or does it contain flashbacks and a muddled time sequence? Can you think why?
- How is the story told? Is it narrated by one of the characters or by an all-seeing ('omniscient') narrator?
- Does the same person tell the story all the way through? Or do we see the events through the minds and feelings of a number of different people?
- Which characters does the narrator like? Which characters do you like or dislike? Do your sympathies change during the course of the book? Why? When?
- Any piece of writing (including your notes and essays) is the result of thousands of choices. No book had to be written in just one way: the author could have chosen other words, other phrases, other characters, other events. How could the author of your novel have written the story differently? If events were recounted by a minor character how would this change the novel?

Studying on your own requires self-discipline and a carefully thought-out work plan in order to be effective. Good luck.

Roddy Doyle was born in Dublin in 1958. He was educated at University College, Dublin, where he graduated with a General Arts degree. After university he taught English and Geography for fourteen years at Greendale Community School in north Dublin. During this time he wrote a political satire, *Your Granny's a Hunger Striker*, which he tried – unsuccessfully – to get Irish and British publishers to accept. He concedes that it was 'a fairly awful book', full of undergraduate humour. However, he continued to write during his teaching career and has now been so successful as a writer that he has left teaching and writes full-time.

His first novel, published in 1987, was *The Commitments*. It was critically acclaimed, and made into a highly successful film by director Alan Parker in 1992. *The Snapper*, Roddy Doyle's second novel, appeared in 1990, and was also subsequently filmed, as was his third novel, *The Van*, which was shortlisted for the Booker Prize in 1991. The three stories, set in Barrytown, a fictional suburb of Dublin, have been published as a collection called *The Barrytown Trilogy*. *Paddy Clarke Ha Ha Ha* was published in 1993, when it won the Booker Prize. The author has since written another novel, *The Woman Who Walked into Doors*, and also published a play called *Brownbread and War*.

Most of Roddy Doyle's writing is about aspects of life in his native Ireland, in particular that of the working-class inhabitants of north Dublin. Doyle appears to have sympathy for Irish working-class culture, although he has been quoted as saying that his own background is lower-middle-class rather than working-class. Themes and characters generally centre on the Irish people, their hopes, dreams and desires, their triumphs and adversities, and what makes them the people they are. He is able to depict vividly the extraordinary inner lives of ordinary people.

*Paddy Clarke Ha Ha Ha* is a beautifully observed portrayal of a boy growing up in 1960s Ireland. It is 1968 when the book opens, and Paddy Clarke is ten, which makes him the same age as the author. It is not unreasonable to guess that elements of the novel are autobiographical, though writers blend their own and others' experiences with the product of their imagination to produce a work of fiction.

Barrytown, where the novel is set, is a fictional suburb of Dublin. In the 1960s it was semi-rural but new building work and developments were rapidly swallowing up the fields and expanding the city towards Barrytown. It is on the east coast of Ireland, and the coastal setting plays an important part in the novel, as does the rapidly developing urbanisation in the effect it has on the lives of the children growing up there.

*The 1960s*

When people think of the 1960s they perhaps think of the phrase 'The Swinging Sixties', which has been bestowed on the decade by the media – it is often portrayed as a decade of wild permissiveness, an exciting sort of non-stop party. In 1968, the London music, film and media world might have been as recent history depicts it, but in most of the north of England and in Ireland, the 'permissive society' had not yet reached local towns and villages. Far from being permissive, Ireland was a Catholic country where old-fashioned family values held sway. Children were taught to respect their parents, teachers and local shopkeepers. Being a Catholic country, 1960s Ireland considered many aspects of the 'permissive society' – such as the contraceptive pill and abortion on demand – to be beyond the pale, and while *Paddy Clarke Ha Ha Ha* is a portrayal of a marriage breaking up, this was still not considered in any way the norm. In one sense, what Roddy Doyle is showing us in his novel is an Ireland which has changed very little by comparison with Britain, and the break-up of his parents' marriage is thus all the more shocking for the hero of the novel.

*Catholicism*    *Paddy Clarke Ha Ha Ha* is not really a novel about the Catholic way of life or the way in which being brought up as Catholics affects the characters' lives; but the fact that Ireland is staunchly Catholic permeates the novel and is present in the many little details which illustrate aspects of Paddy Clarke's life (see also Themes). He mentions Sunday Mass almost in passing as a feature of his existence which is taken for granted. He knows all about Purgatory from Father Moloney, the parish priest, and he toys with the idea of a vocation to the priesthood in the way that virtually all Catholic boys growing up in the 1960s did at some time; it was encouraged at school and church. For the benefit of non-Catholic readers, this York Note will seek to explain from time to time the meaning or significance of various references to the teachings of the Catholic Church.

In the late 1960s Catholics in England and Ireland were beginning to see the effects of the Second Vatican Council, which sought to modernise the teaching of the Church and make it more relevant to contemporary life, for example by replacing the Mass in Latin with Mass in English, or, in Ireland, Gaelic (which is frequently used at Paddy's school; the boys are bilingual). The priests of the 1950s sometimes frightened children with visions of Hell as punishment for mortal sin, and perhaps seemed to talk more about Satan than Jesus, but in the 1960s there was a real drive to stress the more comforting aspects of religious faith like the forgiveness of God. Paddy's upbringing, like that of most Catholic children who grew up in the 1960s, is a mixture of the old-fashioned 'hellfire' approach and the more comforting one.

*Ireland*

Irish history is mentioned more than once in the novel. The 1916 Proclamation of Independence followed the Easter Rising when the Irish declared themselves independent of Britain. Northern Ireland, consisting of six counties, was excepted and remained part of the United Kingdom. This fact, together with the fact that Protestants and Catholics live alongside one another in Northern Ireland, was at the root of the 'troubles' which flared up again in 1969. The Catholic groups sought a solution involving a United Ireland while the Protestant groups maintained the right to keep a Protestant state as part of the United Kingdom. However, the important thing to remember when reading *Paddy Clarke Ha Ha Ha* is that in the 1960s, when the story is set, terrorism of the sort which became commonplace in subsequent decades was non-existent, and many Irish Catholics in the South were quite sympathetic towards the IRA and had been or were activists for a United Ireland. Many Irish Catholics felt that England should have no part of Ireland and should give up the six counties of Northern Ireland, and they were also proud of the Irish history of rejecting the English. It was when acts of terrorism started to affect civilians and the innocent that many Irish people turned against the paramilitary groups and began agitating for peace.

*Home and school*

Paddy Clarke lives in a fictional suburb of Dublin, Barrytown, which is close to the coast of Ireland and, at the time the story opens, is surrounded by farms and open country. As the **narrative** (see Literary Terms) progresses, the city encroaches on Paddy's neighbourhood, with new houses being built almost up to his front door. These houses include those built by 'the Corporation' (similar to council housing in the UK). This suggests that Paddy's background is nearer to Roddy Doyle's own lower-middle-class one than the working-class families he writes about in the *Barrytown Trilogy* (see Roddy Doyle's Background). The neighbourhood is quite a parochial one, with a few shops, no pubs, a church and a primary school. It is the sort of neighbourhood where everyone appears to know everyone else's business. The children at the beginning of the novel have quite a wide-ranging 'territory' for playing games, but as the building work progresses this area gets smaller.

*like growing up*

The primary school which Paddy attends appears to be single-sex; girls are never mentioned. It is a school where Irish as well as English is taught and lessons are often conducted in a mixture of the two languages. It is a Catholic school where the influence of the parish priest is strongly felt. The teachers at the school are treated with a respect which in 1968 was already becoming old-fashioned in parts of England. Mr Hennessey, Paddy's class teacher, is an influential, and sometimes feared, figure in the children's lives (see Characters).

# PART TWO

# SUMMARIES

*Paddy Clarke Ha Ha Ha* has a chaotic, **episodic** (see Literary Terms) structure with no chapter-divisions (see Structure and Language & Style). In this Note the text is treated in four separate sections (based on the Heinemann New Windmills page numbering).

## GENERAL SUMMARY

*Section 1*
*(pp. 1–66)*
*Games and*
*gangs at*
*school and*
*home*

The novel opens with Paddy and his gang coming down the street baiting the neighbours. The gang are introduced: Kevin, who seems to be the leader; Liam and Aidan, whose mother is dead; Ian McEvoy; and Paddy's brother Francis, usually called Sinbad. The gang light fires in the neighbourhood despite Paddy's mother's disapproval, and dodge the watchmen on the local building sites. They put lighter fuel in Sinbad's mouth and light it, burning his lips. Paddy describes games the gang play at the seaside.

There is a brief **flashback** (see Literary Terms) to an earlier period in Paddy's life when he was in trouble with his teacher for lying about his grandfather – Paddy discovers on asking his father that Granda Clarke is dead. Back in the present, we meet Paddy's parents at home when Paddy reads a newspaper headline about World War Three and discusses the news with his father. The history of Ireland is also discussed. Paddy and Sinbad write their letters to Santa with their mother's help. Paddy describes Liam and Aidan's household and their two aunts – their real one, and their widowed father's girlfriend.

Paddy is a collector of facts and we learn some of the strange information he knows. After reading about Father Damien and his life with the lepers on Molokai, Paddy is inspired to invent a game about the priest's life, persuading Sinbad and three younger neighbours to play the parts of the lepers. He tells his parents that he has a vocation to the priesthood, which seems to annoy his father.

Paddy is fascinated by the life of Geronimo, last of the renegade Apache Indians. He describes getting books out of the library; he loves the *Just William* books and has read them all. In imitation of William and his gang, Paddy and his friends paint large Vs on their chests and become the Vigour Tribe. They get into Mrs Kiernan's garden and play with her knickers on the washing line. Later in the week when Paddy is sent to the shop he meets Mrs Kiernan and is terrified of discovery.

Mr Hennessey's class at school is described. Hennessey gives regular spelling and mathematics tests and seats the boys in order of merit. On some Fridays a film is shown in the hall, during which Paddy and his friends get up to mischief; however, they settle down when the films are on because they enjoy them. When the boys kill a rat after watching *The Vikings*, they give it a Viking funeral.

*Section 2
(pp. 67–134)
The
Barrytown
territory*

The game of 'Grand National' is described, in which the boys leap over a row of neighbouring hedges and walls, racing through the gardens and trying to avoid getting caught. Liam breaks his teeth playing. The boys feel guilty about stealing from shops, though they still do it.

Paddy's father brings home a record player and teaches Paddy to sing Hank Williams songs. He also buys a car and teaches himself to drive, and the family take an unsuccessful trip to Dollymount. Paddy is outgrowing his clothes and is pleased at the idea of being as tall as his father. At school there is a medical inspection, and the boys' reactions are described, particularly their fear that their genitals will be examined by a nurse.

In a brief **flashback** (see Literary Terms) Paddy remembers being in his fort under the table when he was younger; then the scene switches to the new building sites in the area and the gang play in the new pipes. Left alone in a pipe with Kevin, Paddy feels close to his friend, until he hits him in the genitals. The gang form a football team and play with other local boys, but they refuse to let the boys from the new Corporation houses play.

Paddy becomes aware that his parents are arguing a lot but Sinbad has not yet noticed.

In one game, the boys have to be named after a swear word for a week. They tire of the game because Kevin always wants to lead it, and they play football instead. Paddy's admiration for George Best is described. His father gives him a book on football. Paddy wants a dog but his father refuses, eventually saying he cannot have a pet because his younger sister Catherine has asthma.

As the building progresses the gang's territory gets smaller and they go further afield on their bikes. Paddy remembers learning to ride his with his father. He describes the gang ruling Bayside on their bikes.

*Section 3 (pp. 134–84) Problems at home*

Paddy becomes increasingly aware of his parents' rows. Meanwhile, Kevin challenges the boys to steal the biggest item from a shop. One day they lift a pile of women's magazines and are seen by Paddy's mother. His father punishes him.

The boys argue over which footballer they want to be in their games; they call themselves Barrytown United and Aidan provides the commentary. As things deteriorate at home, Paddy feels anxiety at the disruption to the normal household routine when one morning the dishes are left undone.

Two boys from the Corporation houses, Seán Whelan and Charles Leavy, join Paddy's class at school. Paddy picks a fight with Seán, during which Charles kicks Paddy unexpectedly. No-one takes Paddy's side. At home he shuts Sinbad into a large suitcase then panics. That night he hears his father hit his mother. Throwing himself into work to try not to think about the row, he ends up at the top desk on Friday.

The gang continue to torment the neighbours. The fights continue at home and Paddy tries to understand his father's interest in the newspapers. He feels that he should keep his parents from fighting by distracting them.

*Section 4*
*(pp. 184–246)*
*Paddy's world*
*falls apart*

When Sinbad's teacher is off sick, Mr Hennessey takes his class and brings him to Paddy because he is crying over his exercise book. Paddy promises not to tell their mother. One day she fails to get up, and the boys have to make their own sandwiches for school. The next day she is better, but Paddy is constantly watchful. Sinbad is now aware of the fights and they discuss them at night. Paddy asks Kevin whether his parents fight, then regrets it and lies about having an aunt and uncle who are always arguing. He plans to run away.

Paddy tries to stay awake all night to prevent the fights, and one day falls asleep in class. Mr Hennessey takes him to the headmaster's office to sleep and afterwards asks him if everything is all right at home. Paddy lies to him and escapes to his friends, who are all eager to help, but he realises that he prefers to be with Sinbad.

Paddy tells himself that his mother's cooking and his dad's spelling tests are just the same, so nothing can be

wrong; but he knows that he is fooling himself. He
seeks the friendship of Charles Leavy, who everyone at
school admires. He wonders why his parents cannot get
on, and imagines his father dying. At school he learns
to appreciate Mr Hennessey's strictness in comparison
with his former teacher.

One evening his father does not come home and Paddy
comforts his mother. The next day he thinks about
playing truant from school with Charles Leavy but
backs out. He has a fight with Kevin which leads to the
break-up of their friendship and a general boycott of
Paddy by his classmates. Paddy is still planning to run
away, but before he can do so his father leaves home for
good. At school the other boys taunt Paddy but he
ignores them. He is the man of the house now.

In the final paragraph, Paddy's father visits him at
Christmas, and they shake hands like two men. Paddy
realises he has had to grow up.

## DETAILED SUMMARIES

### SECTION 1 (PP. 1–66) GAMES AND GANGS AT SCHOOL AND HOME

The novel opens with Paddy Clarke and his gang –
Liam, Aidan, Kevin and Paddy's younger brother
Francis (always called 'Sinbad') – coming down the road
where Paddy lives, and Kevin bashing Mrs Quigley's
gate with a stick. The boys shout 'Quigley' at the gate
before Liam and Aidan turn off down their cul-de-sac.
Paddy notes that their mother is dead, and he and
Kevin agree that it would be 'brilliant' to be in this
position. They are thinking of the time when Liam
dirtied his trousers in class and instead of getting into
trouble with their teacher, Mr Hennessey, he was given
special treatment and taken home to his aunt's house.

Liam insisted afterwards that the teacher had given him a shilling, and he displayed the sweets he had bought with the money.

The boys are trespassing on a building site until Aidan begins running away. They leave Sinbad stuck in the hedge but Paddy is forced to go back for him. At home, there is a discussion about Mr O'Connell, Liam and Aidan's father, who gets drunk and howls at the moon because he misses his wife. When their mother discovers that Sinbad has left a shoe at the building site she is furious and smacks him.

Paddy describes the activities of the gang, lighting fires and writing their names in wet cement all over Barrytown. Usually the names are smoothed over when they return, but sometimes they succeed in putting them there at night, evading the watchman, so that in the morning they have set. They only write their Christian names in the cement in case of discovery.

The gang light a fire and run off when the watchman arrives, but Paddy realises that he has left his jumper on the site, and there is a mad dash to return and rescue it. They shout insults at the watchman and run off before he can catch them. Later they force Sinbad to put lighter fuel in his mouth and set light to it, burning his lips. Paddy says that he prefers lighting fires with magnifying glasses rather than matches, and describes drawing a man on paper and burning him. He digresses to describe cutting paths through the gigantic nettles in the field behind the local shops, and then returns to the subject of the magnifying glass, describing looking at fingerprints with his father.

The barn belonging to Mr Donnelly is set on fire, nothing to do with Paddy's gang. Rumour has it that Mr Donnelly's retarded brother, Uncle Eddie, has been burned to death in the fire, but Paddy's father quickly puts the rumour to rest, describing how he has just met Eddie coming up the road. Sinbad has scabs all over his lips from the burns he has sustained from the lighter fuel.

Paddy describes the games they play at the coast, jumping into the sea shouting 'Voyage To The Bottom Of The Sea' and trying to get as many words out as possible before hitting the water. Kevin is the referee. When Paddy watches the television programme *Voyage To The Bottom Of The Sea* he is scared by the giant jellyfish which swallows the *Seaview*, the submarine featured in the programme. His mother says he is not to watch it again, but by the following week she has forgotten, and anyway there is nothing as frightening again. While at the seaside with Edward Swanwick – who goes to a private school in Dublin and is therefore the butt of the gang's jokes – Paddy encounters a large jellyfish which he thinks has stung him. Terrified, he runs home to his mother, who comforts him in the middle of feeding his two younger sisters, Catherine and the baby Deirdre.

Paddy thinks back to the teacher they had before Mr Hennessey, Miss Watkins. She had once given them a lesson about the Irish Proclamation of Independence in 1916, bringing in a tea-towel illustrating the seven men who had signed the proclamation. On reading that one of the men was called Clarke, Paddy could not resist claiming that the man was his grandfather. The teacher caned him for lying. When he asked his father about Granda Clarke, Paddy's father told him that his grandfather was dead; Paddy had forgotten.

One evening the headline in the newspaper reads 'World War Three Looms Near'. Paddy gets involved in a discussion with his parents, neither of whom takes the headline seriously. His father explains the current

Arab–Israeli conflict to him, particularly the aspect which is apparently cause for concern: that the Americans are backing the Jews and the Russians are backing the Arabs. They also discuss Irish history and the fact that Ireland was not really in the Second World War. Paddy reveals that Kevin's older brother is thinking of joining the reserve army, and Paddy's father reveals pro-United Ireland sympathies.

Paddy and Sinbad are writing their letters to Santa, arguing over the pronunciation of 'Adidas' football boots, which none of their friends will get anyway. Paddy is impatient with Sinbad. He then describes the comfort of his hot water bottle, before digressing to give us a picture of Liam and Aidan's household. The boys are allowed to leap over the worn-out furniture and eat food that Paddy's parents would consider unsuitable, like bacon sandwiches and take-away burgers and chips every night. Paddy has sandwiches for school every day but never eats them, letting them rot in his desk instead, until he is dared to eat one. At home, Sinbad does not eat his dinner (all he likes is bread and jam) and is helped by Paddy.

Paddy describes dusting on Sundays before Mass, and reveals that there are four children in the family although his mother had a baby girl who was stillborn, Angela Mary. Her name is also on the picture of Jesus in the bedroom. He then describes Liam and Aidan's two aunts – their real aunt in Raheny, who makes good biscuits, and his father's new girlfriend, Margaret, who brings the boys sweets and cooks for the family when she comes. Liam and Aidan are sent to Raheny to their aunt's house for a time because Margaret is staying with their father, and Paddy and Sinbad walk there to see them. The four make up rude rhymes about Margaret and Mr O'Connell.

Going downstairs for a drink of water one night, Paddy overhears his parents arguing. He sits on the stairs willing them to stop and they do.

When he reads about Louis Braille, Paddy decides to do his homework essay about his favourite pet in Braille as well as in writing. He asks his father about a pet but is told that he cannot have one. At about this time a mouse is found in the toilet, to Mrs Clarke's horror. Paddy is fascinated but Sinbad is scared when his father flushes it down the toilet.

Kevin and Paddy are both full of curiosity and like to read, but Kevin likes to be the leader; so when Paddy reads about Father Damien and the leper colony of Molokai, he decides not to tell Kevin about the game he plays because Kevin will insist on being Father Damien and Paddy wants this role. He persuades Willy Hancock and the McCarthy twins, who are much younger, to be lepers with Sinbad. Afterwards he worries that the twins or Willy Hancock might get him into trouble with his parents, so he declares that he has a vocation. His parents react differently. Mrs Clarke is absently pleased, but Mr Clarke seems annoyed.

Paddy has a new fascination: Geronimo, last of the renegade Apache Indians. He discusses him with his father, who encourages Paddy to read and often interferes with his choices from the local library. Paddy also likes to read the *Just William* books, and is proud of the fact that he, like William, is in a gang. The gang love to experiment with new words, like 'renegade' and 'vigour'. They draw Vs on their chests one day and call themselves the Vigour Tribe. His mother is curious when she sees the Vs on her sons in the bath, and scrubs them off.

Paddy describes the mischief the gang get up to in Mrs Kiernan's garden, headbutting her knickers on the line.

When he is sent to the local shop for ice-cream that Sunday and meets Mrs Kiernan, he blushes furiously and is terrified of being caught. All the time he is eating his ice-cream he expects her to knock on the door, but she does not.

An incident in class is described, when Ian McEvoy falls asleep. Mr Hennessey punishes him. Hennessey's weekly spelling and mathematics tests are described, with the boys being seated in rank order every Friday. Paddy is usually somewhere near the middle of the class. James O'Keefe drinks the ink and gets up to mischief.

At home, Sinbad is crying one night and Paddy goes downstairs to tell his parents. He becomes aware of further tension between them, but Mrs Clarke comes up to comfort Sinbad – to Paddy's disappointment, as he had been hoping to get his brother into trouble.

Paddy describes the occasional Friday cinema shows in the school hall, which cost threepence each. One Friday Liam and Aidan forget their money and are made to wait until everyone else has gone in. The others tease them about their dad having no money, but they bring it in on the Monday. Paddy can imitate Woody Woodpecker's voice, and does so for the amusement of his friends. Often, if it is sunny, the boys cannot see the film properly because the curtains are not dark enough for a blackout; but when they can see they enjoy Laurel and Hardy, The Three Stooges and various other films, all years out of date. Once the film is *The Vikings*, with music which the boys long to imitate. When Paddy kills a rat they give it a Viking funeral by launching it at sea on a burning piece of wood, and singing the music from the film.

Paddy describes the game he plays of balancing a book on his head going upstairs; if the book falls off he will die. Sinbad tries to imitate him, and one day his father comes out of the bathroom as they are working their way upstairs. He causes Paddy to drop the book.

COMMENT    This first part of the novel consists of chaotic evocations of Paddy's childhood, and sets the scene for the developments which take place in the various relationships between the characters. Most of the **narrative** (see Literary Terms) is about games and mischief. The gang identity is taken for granted from the first sentence: 'We were coming down our road.'

*We are introduced*    Many aspects of Paddy's narration are typical of a
*to the world of a*    ten-year-old child: for example, the assumption that
*ten-year-old child.*  having no mother must be 'brilliant' because you get special treatment from the teachers. The worst thing that can happen in his world is that he gets 'killed', i.e. gets into serious trouble with either his parents or his teachers. Hence the fear and sense of emergency when he leaves his jumper on the building site, especially as he has just seen his younger brother get into trouble for losing a shoe. His attitude to Sinbad is typical of many boys to younger siblings. Sinbad receives dead legs, Chinese burns and, rather more extremely, has lighter fuel fed to him and lit, burning his lips severely. The

one thing which is important to Paddy is that he can 'manage' his younger brother; when they are feeding the lighter fuel to Sinbad, Paddy is worried about losing face in front of the others, especially Kevin, who seems to be the leader.

*Paddy often has to take second place to Kevin in the gang.*

Kevin appears to be Paddy's best friend but the relationship is not an equal one. Kevin is always referee and judge, for example in the game of 'Voyage To The Bottom Of The Sea'. When Paddy wants to play the Father Damien game he knows that if Kevin plays, Kevin will be Father Damien and Paddy will have to be a leper, so he recruits younger boys to play. Kevin is also more daring: it is he who splits his head open diving off the jetty where Paddy and the others do not dare to. When the boys give the rat a Viking burial Paddy has to be the priest because he is useless with matches, while Kevin leads the fire-lighting ceremony.

Paddy tells the story with a typical ten-year-old boy's fascination with snot, excrement, sexual parts and any other conversationally forbidden topics. The boys revel in making up rhymes about the neighbours, even including Liam and Aidan's father, and delight in drawing a naked man on paper and burning his genitals last of all. Paddy is sufficiently ashamed of these enthusiasms, however, not to want his parents to find out. Though the gang have a hilarious time headbutting Mrs Kiernan's knickers when they get into her garden, Paddy is truly terrified of discovery when he meets her in the shop the following Sunday. He delights in mischief and loves to see others get into trouble – for example when Ian McEvoy falls asleep in class and is punished by Mr Hennessey – but he has a healthy respect for parents, teachers and the parish priest. The boys may shout insults at the neighbours and the watchmen on the building sites, but they are

*Paddy and his friends are careful to avoid getting caught.*

careful not to be caught, only writing their Christian names in the wet cement, for example.

Paddy enjoys an affectionate relationship with both his parents, though he fears his father finding out about any misdemeanours far more than he does his mother. He goes to his mother for comfort (for example, when he thinks he has been stung by the jellyfish) and helps her with household tasks such as dusting. He talks to his father on a wide range of subjects including the news, current affairs, Irish history, books and famous people like Geronimo.

*The boys are often quite cruel to each other.* While Paddy looks up to Kevin and considers him to be the leader, the two of them tease Liam and Aidan, especially about their widowed father's girlfriend and their home circumstances. The boys are quite cruel to each other; Paddy thinks up the idea of teasing Liam and Aidan about not having their money for the Friday picture show, and they keep saying it until Aidan cries. Paddy also enjoys teasing Edward Swanwick, who is not in their gang, and baits Sinbad unmercifully, assisted by Kevin.

Paddy is obviously a bright boy; he reads voraciously and collects information, which he interjects into his account of games and mischief whenever it seems at all relevant. He becomes passionately interested in whatever he reads about – Father Damien one week and Geronimo the next – and often introduces into the gang games connected with whatever he has read or seen on television or film – the Viking funeral, fingerprinting based on *The Man from UNCLE*, or the *Voyage To The Bottom Of The Sea* game. He has a lively imagination and lives passionately in his own world of the gang and their games.

Paddy is also fascinated with words, especially new ones such as 'renegade' and 'vigour' (which inspires a week of

being the Vigour Tribe), and definitions, making the
others laugh by repeating the dictionary definition of
Association Football when they are playing in the
street.

GLOSSARY        **gick** (colloquial) faeces

**codding** hoaxing

**The Corporation** the local authority, similar to local councils in
the UK

**mickey** (colloquial) penis

**hurley** stick used for playing hurling (a game similar to hockey
and lacrosse)

**Voyage To The Bottom Of The Sea** 1960s television adventure
series about the submarine *The Seaview*

**gee** (colloquial) female genitalia

**spa** (colloquial) short for 'spastic', used as an insult by the
boys

**Woody Woodpecker** cartoon character, used to introduce
children's cinema screenings during the 1950s and 1960s

**Napoleon Solo** hero of the 1960s television series *The Man
from UNCLE*

**F.C.A.** Forsa Cosanta Aitúil: the Irish reserve army, similar to
the Territorial Army in the UK

**the Guards** the Irish police force

**eccer** homework

**eejit** (colloquial) idiot

## A Identify the speaker.

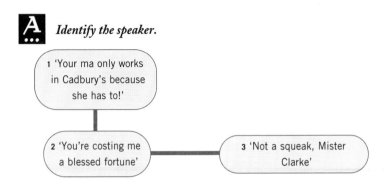

1 'Your ma only works in Cadbury's because she has to!'

2 'You're costing me a blessed fortune'

3 'Not a squeak, Mister Clarke'

## Identify 'to what or whom' this comment refers.

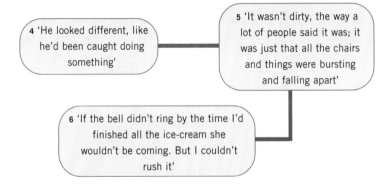

4 'He looked different, like he'd been caught doing something'

5 'It wasn't dirty, the way a lot of people said it was; it was just that all the chairs and things were bursting and falling apart'

6 'If the bell didn't ring by the time I'd finished all the ice-cream she wouldn't be coming. But I couldn't rush it'

Check your answers on page 95.

## B Consider these issues.

a The differences between his father's and his mother's attitudes when Paddy says he has a vocation.

b The reasons why Liam and Aidan put up with the other boys' sometimes cruel treatment of them.

c Whether you find Paddy a likeable character.

d The way Roddy Doyle uses dialogue (see Literary Terms) to create a vivid picture of the lives of Paddy and his friends.

section $2$ (pp. 67–134) the barrytown territory

The game of 'Grand National' is described by Paddy:
the boys, as 'horses', run through a row of neighbouring
gardens, jumping walls, fences and hedges, to end in
the Hanleys' garden at the end of the row. The
Hanleys' is the most dangerous because Mr Hanley is
retired and takes great pride in his garden, spending a
lot of time there. In a digression, Paddy tells the reader
about the time he got into trouble with his parents
because Mrs Quigley complained about him and Kevin
breaking her window. He was made to stay in his
bedroom and reflect on his misdemeanours until he was
terrified of the physical punishment to come from his
father, and ready to tell the truth. He reflects that it
was Kevin and not he who broke the window, though
they were both blamed.

At Sinbad's first Holy Communion there is a family
gathering at Paddy's aunt and uncle's house and Paddy
sings songs that his father has taught him. There is a
reflection on the teaching of the Catholic Church
which Paddy and his brother are receiving at school,
church and home. If you die in mortal sin you go to
Hell, but lesser (or 'venial') sins merit a time in
Purgatory. Paddy explains the tariff for various
wrongdoings, the most notable of which, as he sees it,
is stealing a copy of *Football Monthly* – four million
years in Purgatory! All of this is explained to the boys
by Father Moloney, who comes into school on the first
Wednesday of every month.

Paddy's father teaches him to sing Hank Williams
songs and traditional Irish ballads. The family's small
record collection is described. Mr Clarke's next
acquisition is a black Cortina, in which he teaches
himself to drive. There is a family excursion in the new
car to Dollymount, a place only walking distance from

their house. Paddy cannot understand why they don't go to the mountains and make a day of it. During the 'picnic' – they eat in the car because it is raining – there is obvious tension between his parents, and he and Sinbad fight over their shared can of Fanta while Mrs Clarke gets out of the car with Catherine. She then quickly returns, saying it was too wet for Cathy. It is clear that something has happened which the boys do not quite understand.

Paddy is growing too tall for his trousers and he is pleased at the thought of being as tall as his father. He is horrified when his mother fastens the trousers with a safety pin but she assures him it is just for that day. At school there is a medical inspection which is described in detail, especially the way in which the first two boys in, Brian Sheridan and James O'Keefe, tease the others still waiting and make them expect all kinds of horrors. The worst part, apparently, is that a nurse looks at the boys' genitals, and Paddy dreads this in an agony of embarrassment while he waits. However, when he and Kevin go in it is not as bad as expected.

In a brief **flashback** (see Literary Terms) Paddy describes the fort he used to have under the living room table when he was younger, and how he hid from the rest of the family for hours. Abruptly he returns to the present and describes the gang playing in the huge water pipes being laid on the new building sites. Running through the main pipe is the most dangerous thing so that is what the gang do. Kevin has them all worried by hiding in the pipe, and Paddy goes in to find him there, safe. The two of them are fellow conspirators and the closest of friends for a few minutes, until Kevin 'prunes' Paddy, grabbing his genitals roughly. This practice is forbidden in school and Paddy tells us how James O'Keefe got into trouble with the headmaster for doing it.

The building work is changing the territory in which
the Clarkes live and the boys play; for a while Mr
Clarke has to park his new car at the local shops
because there is no proper road outside their house.
One day Mrs Kilmartin at the shop becomes angry with
Mrs Clarke because the car is left there, and this causes
further tension between Paddy's parents. The pipe
becomes too long to run through, while many of the
local farms are altered forever, with hedgerows being
ploughed up. A new railway bridge is built, which leads
the gang to speculate as to whether or not the old one
will be blown up and whether it is true that two men
have been killed by the building of the new one.

Alan Baxter has a Scalextric car set, with which Paddy
and his friends long to play, but they are kept outside
the house, looking in through the window. Only Kevin
is allowed in to watch, because his older brother is a
friend of Alan's. With some envy, Paddy describes
Martin, Kevin's older brother, and his friend Terence
Long and the trouble they get into. Their building of
huts in the hills inspires the gang to imitate them, and
they make booby traps until Ian McEvoy cuts his foot
on one and is taken to hospital. Paddy insists that the
trap, which is made from wire rather than the string
the gang use, has been put there by boys from the
Corporation houses, who he hates. When he calls them
'slum scum' his mother is angry with him. This does
nothing to change the gang's attitude to the boys from
the Corporation houses, who are not allowed to join in
their football games.

As the new roads are laid, the gang trap bees in the tar
with ice-pop sticks. They speculate on the fate of a
local man said to have died when a bee flew into his
mouth and stung him. Paddy reflects on getting an
earwig in his mouth and how it reminded him of a
story about a man who died because a lizard made a

nest inside his stomach, which his mother tells him is nonsense. Shortly afterwards Paddy becomes aware of an argument between his parents and he and Sinbad distract their father from it.

Paddy describes the gang's latest game. Kevin is the high priest, wielding a poker. The boys chant new words they have learned and are fascinated by, and each boy is named after a swear word for a week. Paddy becomes 'Fuck', a fact which the boys all remember even though they usually forget who is supposed to be which word. The game comes to an end because the others are tired of Kevin always being the high priest and of being hit – often quite violently – with the poker.

They turn to football instead, finding new places to play as the building work changes their territory. Paddy tells us how he received a book about football as a present from his father, with what he thought was George Best's autograph at the front. He describes his disappointment when – a year later – he discovered that his father had deceived him about the authenticity of the signature.

Various aspects of Paddy's home life are detailed. The family keep the front room as their 'drawing room', unlike some of his friends' families. When Paddy and Sinbad lead the family discussion round to pets and make another attempt to persuade their father to get them a dog, he gives them a conclusive answer: they cannot have a pet because Catherine has asthma.

The territory of the gang is steadily decreasing as the building work proceeds, and Paddy cuts his foot playing on the dumps between the new roads. The gang take to their bikes and extend their territory north to Bayside. Paddy describes how his father taught him to ride his bike. At Bayside, the boys play knocking on doors and riding away. Paddy reflects on scabs and sticky eyes.

COMMENT    During this section the reader is treated to a lively and undifferentiated account of the gang's games and territory, with the ten-year-olds' obsession with snot, swear words and excrement evident throughout. We laugh at many of the boys' mischievous exploits. Grand National is described with tremendous pace and excitement except when Liam breaks his teeth – the ones he is 'supposed to have for the rest of his life' – and Paddy is clearly horrified, so much so that the other

*The boys do not*     boys don't run away, which is what they normally do
*usually stick up for*  when someone falls, in case they all get caught and
*each other.*         blamed for any damage.

The cruelty of young boys towards each other is evident; being in a gang does not mean that you wish to share in the trouble caused, and any boy who can get away does so. As usual, Kevin is slightly more daring than the rest, which is why Paddy looks up to him, and it is Kevin who breaks Mrs Quigley's window, even though Paddy is punished by his father for having been there. Liam has broken his teeth falling out of the most dangerous hedge in the row, the Hanleys'. Laurence Hanley, one of the two unmarried adult sons of the house, is described as 'evil' by Paddy. All adults whose

*Paddy often feels guilty for wrongdoing.*

windows are broken and hedges and gardens invaded are, of course, 'evil' in the minds of Paddy and his friends. They delight in making up salacious details about the sex lives of their neighbours and demonising them. The women are all 'witches' and the men impotent or fat and useless.

The Catholic background against which Paddy's adventures are played out (see also Context & Setting and Themes) is explored in this section. Paddy's commentary on pages 73–6 is a breathless verbatim account of his thoughts on sin and punishment, gleaned from his family, friends, teachers and the parish priest Father Moloney, who comes into school monthly to talk to Paddy's class as well as preaching at Sunday Mass. The reader is amused to see how literally Paddy and his brother interpret what they are taught, and how seriously they take the whole concept of Purgatory, for example. It is touching to see how Paddy worries about the fate of his stillborn sister.

*Mrs Clarke stops her husband teaching Paddy 'I'm Gonna Wash That Man Right Out of My Hair' for fear that Paddy might sing it outside the home (p. 78).*

Other aspects of Paddy's education outside school are explored when his father's record collection and the singing are described. Mr Clarke's eccentricity is revealed, as is the easy-going atmosphere in the Clarke household and Paddy's sudden realisation that what a family finds entertaining in the privacy of their home might not seem relevant or appropriate in school and outside the home. Paddy clearly loves his father's eccentricity, especially when he buys the car and teaches himself to drive, singing the *Batman* music: 'he was mad sometimes, brilliant mad' (p. 79). Mrs Clarke clearly does not share Paddy's enthusiasm for her husband's erratic driving, and when the picnic takes place the tension between the parents becomes obvious to Paddy. Clearly, Dollymount is chosen because Mr Clarke lacks the confidence to drive further afield, but Mrs Clarke needs 'a decent day out'. The antics of

Paddy and Sinbad in the back of the car are amusing
and typical of children on family outings: arguing over
sandwiches and drinks, demanding the toilet before
they have travelled half a mile, making farting noises
with their arms, and so on. Mrs Clarke disapproves of
their obsession with excrement and obscenity in
general; she will not let them call the Marietta biscuits
'botty bickies' (p. 83). During the picnic, when his
mother gets out of the car in the rain with Catherine,
Paddy becomes aware that 'something had happened'
which he does not yet understand but finds vaguely
disturbing. This is one of the early signs that all is not
well in the relationship between Mr and Mrs Clarke.

Like every ten-year-old, Paddy dreads medical
inspection at school. The horror inspired in the others
by the first two boys who see the nurse is portrayed
in a highly amusing **set piece** (see Literary Terms), and
the reader will perhaps **empathise** (see Literary Terms)
with their plight. Worst of all, the boys' genitals are to
*The boys' fear of* be inspected. Though Paddy and the gang find it highly
*the medical* amusing to make up rhymes and be obsessed with jokes
*inspection is* about sex, excrement and genitals, they are deeply
*amusing but very* embarrassed at actually dealing with intimate matters,
*real.* and a female nurse inspecting ten-year-olds' bodies is
guaranteed to have them in an agony of embarrassment
and fear which is clearly conveyed to the reader. Paddy
remembers the safety pin in his trousers too late when
he gets into the medical room, but at least his
underwear is clean, unlike Kevin's. Paddy's comments
on the homes, meals and clothing of his friends are
simply made as factual observations, but the reader
becomes aware as the story progresses that Paddy's
family has high standards of discipline, nutrition and
cleanliness which are not shared by the families of all
his friends. Paddy seems to become aware of this at
times with a kind of surprised shock.

Again the exploits of the gang are described in amusing detail – running through the water pipes, playing with tar, building huts and dens and setting booby traps. So vivid are the descriptions that we can imagine the places in the gang's territory clearly and almost feel part of their games. Also vividly evoked is the longing the boys feel for the new, expensive and coveted toy, the Scalextric set, and the frustration of only being allowed to watch the older boys playing with it from outside.

*Martin and Terence are more daring than Paddy's gang.*

Paddy describes the exploits of Martin, Kevin's brother, and his friend Terence Long, with a mixture of amusement and envy. The boys get up to worse things than Paddy dares, which is perhaps the reason for Kevin's greater daring and leadership of the gang. In his description, Paddy will never admit that he is not as hard as the older boys, but the envy is conveyed to the reader when he writes of Martin: 'I thought he was brilliant. Kevin did too but he hated him as well' (p. 101). In these sentences the relationship between older and younger brothers is summed up. Sinbad

*Paddy's attitude towards Sinbad is mixed.*

clearly feels the same way about Paddy, but Paddy's attitude to his younger brother contains a mixture of affection, irritation and the feeling that to fail to force Sinbad to do quite unreasonable things such as be buried in mud or swallow lighter fuel is to lose face with Kevin and the rest of the gang. The boys treat Aidan, Liam's younger brother, in the same way, and occasionally Kevin and Paddy pick on Liam, who is more vulnerable than they are because of the loss of his mother and the rather erratic home life he and Aidan have, shunted between Mr O'Connell and his girlfriend, and their aunt in Raheny.

Other obsessions of the gang are described, such as the horrified fascination with death, especially the dreadful stories which circulate about unusual death. The man with the bee in his mouth is one example; and which primary school gang has not listened with fascinated horror to a tale like the one about the man in Africa who ate a salad and then died from a lizard's nest in his stomach? Paddy uses this as an excuse not to eat his salad, but his mother is having none of it and abruptly deflates the story.

One of the most amusing **set pieces** (see Literary Terms) in the book is the swear word game (pp. 111–16). Many of the boys' intense fascinations with new words, swearing, the forbidden, and the nature of their friendships and gang life are revealed in it. The boys are round a fire, sufficiently far away from the shops not to be overheard, which indicates that they know adults would disapprove of their activities and language. Kevin, as always, is in charge; he is the only one allowed to wield the poker and give out the punishments. The boys begin by chanting new words they have learned in class and find fascinating: 'trellis', 'banjaxed', 'substandard'. Many of them come from Mr Hennessey. The excitement and terror of 'the real ceremony' – not knowing who is next to be hit with the poker and is going to have to think of a swear word to become for the week – is clearly conveyed. Also clear is the agony and rage of Liam, hit twice for crying out with pain instead of swearing, and then the isolation he feels when he leaves. Despite the insult to his dead mother uttered by Kevin, Liam's brother Aidan stays in the circle, as do all the other boys. It is better to stay and endure what Kevin doles out than to be the outsider. In a stark sentence the cruelty of young boys is revealed: 'It was good being in the circle, better than where Liam was going' (p. 115). Paddy is immensely proud of being 'Fuck', the best word. The boys' reluctance to shout the word is amusing, as is their awe of uttering it in a public place. The boys are supposed to use their names all week, but they usually forget who

*There is a slightly sinister edge to the swear word game.*

has appropriated which word. The reader is amused that on this occasion, however, Paddy can write with pride: 'I was Fuck though. They all remembered that' (p. 116). The game comes to a premature end because the rest of the gang become tired of being hit with the poker by Kevin, with no prospect of getting a turn at being leader. Paddy, showing loyalty to Kevin as ever, accompanies him to the seafront the next Friday and pretends that he wanted the game to continue.

The incident in which Paddy realises that his father has lied to him about George Best's autograph is a turning point in his relationship with his father; he realises for the first time that his father is not infallible and is capable of a falsehood. In some ways the situation is worse than if Mr Clarke had simply said that the signature was printed, because he makes up an elaborate lie about George Best signing autographs, thinking that he is pleasing his son, but is caught out by Paddy's intense questioning. Paddy's eventual realisation that the signature is printed makes him feel foolish for having half-believed his father.

*Paddy rarely mentions his sisters.*

When Mr Clarke tells Paddy and Sinbad clearly and firmly that they cannot have a dog or any other pet because of Catherine's asthma, it is the first time that Paddy is forced to acknowledge the existence of his sisters. They do not feature prominently in the novel because to a ten-year-old boy, a baby girl and a toddler are insignificant. Paddy never speaks to Catherine because she is 'useless' (p. 126). There is a veiled resentment in Paddy's statement that the boys are not allowed to talk about Catherine's asthma, but at the same time a complete acceptance of things as they are in the family. By the end of this section, Paddy is starting to reflect on his family and their life together, and to realise that things are not always as he would wish them to be. He is vaguely aware of tensions,

especially between his parents, but does not really
understand what they are about.

GLOSSARY    **Purgatory** in Catholic teaching, a place or state between Heaven
            and Hell in which the souls of those who have died expiate
            their sins before going to Heaven
            **venial sin** a sin which is regarded as relatively minor, involving
            only a partial loss of grace
            **Limbo** in Catholic teaching, the eternal abode of unbaptised
            infants
            **Artane** the local borstal
            **crack** fun
            **B.C.G.** vaccine against tuberculosis
            **mitched** (dialect) played truant
            **Dinkies** Dinky cars, toys popular in the 1960s

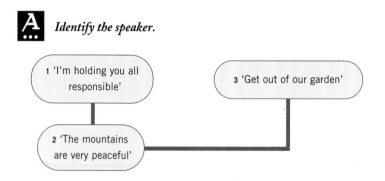

**A** *Identify the speaker.*

1 'I'm holding you all responsible'

3 'Get out of our garden'

2 'The mountains are very peaceful'

*Identify 'to what or whom' this comment refers.*

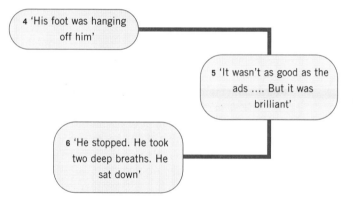

4 'His foot was hanging off him'

5 'It wasn't as good as the ads .... But it was brilliant'

6 'He stopped. He took two deep breaths. He sat down'

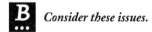
Check your answers on page 95.

**B** *Consider these issues.*

a The way Kevin rules the gang.

b How Paddy gradually begins to realise that there is tension between his parents, starting with the trip to Dollymount.

c The ways in which the boys' lives are influenced by the changes in the landscape of Barrytown.

d How the small details in the descriptions of Paddy's home and school life add to your enjoyment of the story.

section 3 (pp. 134–84) problems at home

Paddy realises that he alone knows the extent of his parents' fighting and the constant tension between them. Sinbad only notices when there are shouts and screams. The tension begins to affect Paddy's behaviour at Sunday breakfast.

Paddy describes more of the gang's mischief, this time stealing from shops and, on one occasion, forcing Edward Swanwick to eat some Persil soap powder which they have stolen. The boys do not shoplift in Barrytown for fear of their parents, but choose shops further afield between Raheny and Baldoyle. Mrs Kilmartin is too efficient and Mr Fitz too nice to be robbed. Tootsie, however, is a particular target because she does not appear to be aware that the boys might steal from her. Kevin runs a competition to get the biggest box, which must be full (this rule is stipulated after Liam gets an empty one). One day, grabbing a pile of *Woman's Way* magazines from the shop in Raheny, Paddy catches sight of his mother out with the pram. He is terrified that she has seen him. Later he gets home and discovers that she has reported it to his father, and he is in deep trouble. Mr Clarke beats Paddy and Sinbad with his belt and they comfort each other under their blankets in bed by having a mock fight.

An era seems to Paddy to come to an end one day, when his mother puts the multicoloured venetian blinds in the bath to wash them and their colours change.

The gang's football pitch in the fields has been built over so they are forced to play football in the road. Each boy picks a football player to be, and Aidan is the commentator. The side Sinbad is on are given a

two-goal lead because of his youth, but in fact he is a
fine player and his team usually win. Paddy reassesses
his brother as well as Liam and Aidan during this
section. Aidan shows an unexpected sense of humour
when he commentates. The boys decide, with some
help from James O'Keefe's father, to call themselves
Barrytown United.

Paddy describes spinning round in the garden until he
makes himself sick, straight after dinner. He reflects on
what he has been told about the dangers of swimming
after a meal, mentioning that when he went in the
water up to his belly button the sea did not feel any
different.

The next morning, when the boys get up, the previous
day's washing-up has not been done and the table has
not been cleared; this worries Paddy because it is not
like his mother to forget. Sometimes he and Sinbad
wash up but he remembers that it is Thursday and the
previous evening was not their night for washing up.
His parents have had one of their quiet fights.

At school, there are two new boys from the hated
Corporation estate. Paddy and some of his friends are
angry to find that the boys, Seán Whelan and Charles
Leavy, are in their class instead of the lower ability
group. Kevin is dared to say as much to Mr Hennessey
but in the end does not. Seán is seated beside David
Geraghty, a boy with polio who tends to be avoided by
the others, and Charles is put next to Liam, which
causes Kevin and Paddy to ostracise Liam too. While
watching Seán and his glasses case, Paddy is hit by Mr
Hennessey for inattention, and consequently he swears
revenge on Seán. After school, Kevin pushes Paddy into
a fight with Seán. The fight is closely matched, though
Paddy feels he is winning, until suddenly Charles Leavy
joins in and kicks Paddy. No-one supports Paddy, to

his surprise and anguish, and a workman has to intervene and stop the fight.

At home, Paddy shuts Sinbad into the large leather suitcase under the bed in their room. At first Paddy intends to leave him in there for a short while before letting him out, but panics when he cannot hear any sound from his brother and tells his father, who comes upstairs and lets Sinbad out. As he reflects on the fact that Sinbad made no fuss, Paddy is forced to realise that his younger brother is growing up and that perhaps 'Sinbad' is no longer an appropriate name for him. Sinbad gives up the night-light that has always been acknowledged as being for him, though it is in the bedroom shared by both boys, and Paddy realises that he too has enjoyed the comfort of the light and is scared at times without it.

One night, Paddy is listening to his parents arguing in the kitchen after Sinbad has gone to bed, when he hears a sound he recognises, almost disbelievingly, as a smack. His father has hit his mother. Mrs Clarke runs upstairs to her room, and after a minute Mr Clarke leaves the house.

Paddy feels he has to protect his mother, so he stays awake as late as he can each night, splashing cold water

on his pyjamas to keep himself awake, and spending as
long as he can on his homework in order to delay
his bedtime. He now asks his mother rather than his
father to check his spellings. However, his father insists
on checking them and he gets one wrong deliberately,
though he does not himself know why. After a week
of this extra work, Paddy scores the top marks in his
class and is moved up to the top desk on Friday.

After school the gang play in a new trench which has
glutinous mud at the bottom. Aidan gets stuck in the
mud and begins to sink. At first the boys think it is
funny, but eventually Paddy begins to worry, as he did
with Sinbad in the suitcase, and Liam runs off for his
father, who returns with a ladder to get Aidan out.
Paddy reflects on the fact that Liam and Aidan
sometimes miss school and play outdoors instead.

A local boy called Keith Simpson drowns in a pond,
which upsets the whole community; Mrs Clarke cries at
news of his death, which leads Paddy to imagine that
they must be related.

When the gang are talking about 'hari-kari', Kevin
grabs Ian McEvoy's arm and twists it behind his
back, and Liam tells him to stop. Paddy waits for
Kevin to put Liam in his place, but instead he seems
annoyed with Paddy for interrupting and contradicting
him.

Kevin, Paddy, Sinbad and Ian are caught stealing
sawdust from the butcher, and he demonstrates slicing
a chop from a leg of beef with his knife, explaining that
he will do the same to the boys if he catches them
stealing again. Terrified, they escape. Ian's guinea-pig
dies after a cold night, and he blames his mother for
refusing to let him take the animal to bed with him.
The gang use Ian's sister's doll to make an image of
Mrs McEvoy to stick pins in and curse. It has no effect,

of course. They squash the dead guinea-pig through the Kilmartins' letter box.

At home the rows continue, and Paddy reflects on the fact that his mother does most of the listening, as well as answering her husband's arguments at greater length. He also reflects on the nature of fathers, who, it seems, do not wish to be disturbed when they are watching television or reading the newspaper – except for Mr O'Connell, and Paddy does not want a father like him. He realises that his own parents look after him and his siblings in a way that Liam and Aidan's father fails to do. Paddy wins a medal in a race at school and dashes home to tell his father, only to be sent away because Mr Clarke is reading the paper. However, Mr Clarke apologises to Paddy and praises him. Paddy finds his father's behaviour much more inconsistent than his mother's and is never quite sure of his mood. Paddy reflects at length on newspapers – their inaccuracy, their boring nature and their habit of absorbing his father's attention.

An argument can now start in the Clarke household over the slightest matter, even an innocent observation by Mrs Clarke about the shopping. Paddy attempts to distract his parents before a real row starts by asking to watch television, though he does not know what is on. Giving permission, Mr Clarke asks about Paddy's homework and spellings, and when he cracks a joke about the word 'centenary' Paddy laughs with relief, a laugh which almost turns into a cry. He is sent to bed happy, because he has deflected the anger and the row.

COMMENT    Prior to this section Paddy has been only vaguely aware of tension and conflict between his parents, but from here onwards the situation begins to affect his daily life to a greater extent and to colour his reactions to events. Staying awake for half the night, willing his parents not

to fight, is a symptom of this awareness, as is the time
he spends on his homework, hoping to prevent a fight
starting by being present in the kitchen. The scene in
which Paddy hears the smacking sound and realises that
his father has hit his mother is a shock both to him and
to the reader, who follows Paddy's view of events so
closely.

*Paddy senses the
passage of time.*

When Mrs Clarke washes the venetian blinds and
Paddy begs her to leave one slat of each colour
uncleaned, there is a sense that he is trying desperately
to keep things as they were when he was a little
younger and to avoid the changes he fears might come
about if the tension gets any worse. He is not sure what
these changes might be and has not even begun to
speculate, but he seems to want to prevent any change
and make time stand still. However, the fact that time
will not halt is emphasised when one morning the
washing-up is not done by Mrs Clarke because of a
fight the night before.

To a great extent, though, the games and activities of
the gang continue as normal, with the game of stealing
the biggest box from a shop, although even this is
tinged with disaster (in a way that the swear word
game, for example, is not) because Mrs Clarke catches
the boys and Mr Clarke punishes them. Paddy becomes
more aware of relationships between the boys and the
ways in which they can shift; for example, he reflects on
Liam's attempt to stand up to Kevin and the way in
which Kevin dominates the others and decides who is
approved of and who is not.

*How does the
author convey the
excitement of the
football match?*

There is another fine **set piece** (see Literary Terms) in
the gang's football game, with Aidan as commentator.
Paddy points out that Aidan is never usually as funny or
droll as he is when commentating on the match, and
during the match Paddy is forced to reflect on and
re-appraise both Aidan and Sinbad, who is a natural

footballer although none of the older boys will admit it.

Paddy's fascination with bodily functions continues, but he seems more intent upon punishing himself in this section. Instead of reflecting on sticky eyes, snot and scabs, he attempts to make himself sick by spinning round in the garden and thinks about how a full stomach can result in drowning; the gang, meanwhile, talk of suicide attempts and 'hari-kari'. There is a slightly more destructive edge to many of the things they do in this section of the book:

- Aidan is nearly hurt in the muddy trench, and the gang break a childish code when Liam is allowed to go for adult help in the form of his father.
- The incident when the boys steal sawdust from the butcher has a sinister overtone, as he demonstrates slicing chops off a cow's leg with a knife, and threatens to do the same to the boys if they are caught stealing from him again.
- Even the amusing incident of the gang sticking pins in a doll to harm Ian McEvoy's mother in revenge for letting the guinea-pig die seems more sinister than the antics they got up to earlier in the novel.
- The stuffing of the dead guinea-pig through the Kilmartins' door completes the slightly darker nature of the mischief.

There is some sense that the gang is getting slightly out of hand.

It is clear that Paddy's parents are becoming absorbed by the conflict between them to the extent that he and Sinbad do not get as much attention as usual. The boys make sometimes desperate attempts to keep things 'normal' between their parents by cracking idiotic jokes and telling stories about minor misdemeanours of children at school in order to distract them from arguing.

The fact that even Sinbad now joins in these attempts
shows the extent to which both boys are being affected
by the atmosphere at home. At one point in this
section, the tension has an unexpected and good effect
on Paddy: the extra hours he spends on homework (in
order to postpone his bedtime and the inevitable row
which will follow) lead to his highest ever achievements
at school and to his scoring so well that he is promoted
to the top desk for the week. He is plainly pleased by
this, as he rushes home to tell his parents, but it is sad
that he has only achieved it by his desperation to keep
his parents from fighting.

GLOSSARY          **blemming** kicking hard and fast
                  **Hari-kari** suicide pact traditionally said to be made by Japanese
                      soldiers
                  **snailers** (colloquial) trails of mucus from a child's nose
                  **Fianna Fail** and **Fine Gael** Irish political parties
                  **The Virginian** 1960s cowboy series on TV

# TEST YOURSELF (SECTION 3)

**A** *Identify the speaker.*

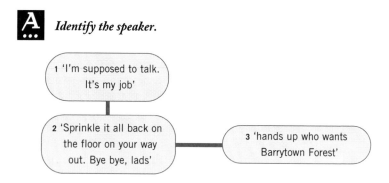

1 'I'm supposed to talk. It's my job'

2 'Sprinkle it all back on the floor on your way out. Bye bye, lads'

3 'hands up who wants Barrytown Forest'

## Identify the person 'to whom' this comment refers.

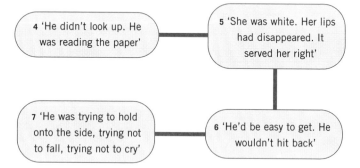

4 'He didn't look up. He was reading the paper'

5 'She was white. Her lips had disappeared. It served her right'

7 'He was trying to hold onto the side, trying not to fall, trying not to cry'

6 'He'd be easy to get. He wouldn't hit back'

Check your answers on page 95.

**B** *Consider these issues.*

a How Paddy feels about his father when he discovers that he has lied about George Best's signature.

b How Paddy gradually becomes aware that things are wrong between his parents.

c The role of the two 'Corporation boys', Charles and Seán, in this part of the novel.

d How the author creates the impression of Paddy becoming less active and more of an observer in this section.

SECTION 4 (PP. 184–246) PADDY'S WORLD FALLS APART

One morning in school two of the teachers are off sick
so Mr Hennessey has to take care of another class
besides his own. He leaves Paddy's class with plenty of
long division sums to do. While Kevin causes trouble
pretending to draw on another pupil's book, Paddy
happily gets on with his work, as he likes this task.
Suddenly Mr Hennessey returns to the room and holds
an exercise book in front of Paddy. It is Sinbad's, and it
is streaked with tear stains – Sinbad has cried all over
his exercise book while Mr Hennessey has been taking
his class. Mr Hennessey tells Paddy that he is to tell
their mother about the incident, but Paddy later
promises Sinbad that he will not say anything at home.

Soon afterwards, Mrs Clarke fails to get up one
morning when the boys get up for school. Paddy's
father goes to ask Mrs McEvoy to look after the baby
girls for the day, and Paddy and Sinbad are left to get
their own breakfasts and make their own lunches for
school. Paddy pushes Sinbad's face close to the gas
when making them both toast. Paddy suspects that his
mother is not really sick, but his father's calm manner
when he returns from the McEvoys' house allays his
fears. The boys get crisp sandwiches for lunch. On the
way home from school they look for a local man that
the boys call 'the Weirdy Fella'. Kevin has left school
early because his grandmother is dying and Paddy is
secretly relieved at his absence.

The next day Mrs Clarke gets up in her dressing gown.
Paddy is relieved to see that she is much better, but
he stays awake for most of the night just to make
sure. By the next morning she seems her usual self.
At school Paddy goes to the shops for Mr Hennessey
and is treated to the change, with which he buys a
gobstopper. While he is putting the sweet in his mouth

James O'Keefe's mother arrives at school to accuse Mr Hennessey of picking on her son. The teacher and the parent disappear to talk things over, and afterwards Mr Hennessey is really nice to the class.

Paddy notices that his parents fight all the time now, with one row seeming to blend into another. He tries to share his anguish about it with Sinbad in bed one night. Sinbad reveals that he prefers to be called by his real name, Francis. Paddy resolves to look after his younger brother.

Paddy observes his parents while they watch television, particularly the news. The Vietnam War is featured and his father shows impatience with politicians. Paddy misunderstands the term 'guerrillas', thinking it is 'gorillas', which amuses his father immensely.

One day, in a desperate attempt to find out if he is alone in his suffering, he asks Kevin whether or not his parents ever fight, and immediately regrets it. Kevin says that his parents argue, and Paddy, anxious to avoid questioning, invents an uncle and aunt who have frightening rows. He then worries about Kevin telling his mother and Kevin's mother reporting what Paddy has said to Mrs Clarke. He realises that he should have asked Liam instead, and tries to tell Kevin that he was only joking. He resolves to run away from home.

Mr Hennessey leaves the class to get on with some work from their atlases, having noticed that Paddy's eyes are red and said that he looks as if he has not had enough sleep. Paddy reflects that this is because he has succeeded in staying awake for the entire night. Before the dawn, the grey light had frightened him, and he had been surprised to hear a cockerel crow. Paddy falls asleep over his work, and is discovered by Mr Hennessey when he returns.

Mr Hennessey carries him to the headmaster's room,
where he is allowed to sleep. When Paddy wakes
up he is surprised and embarrassed, and escapes back
to his class as soon as the headmaster dismisses him.
Even Kevin does not say anything to him, and the
others appear to think that he is sick and keep a
respectful distance. At the end of afternoon school
Mr Hennessey keeps Paddy behind and asks him
whether there is anything wrong at home. Paddy lies to
him, saying that everything is all right. When he gets
outside his friends are eager to help him with copying
down the homework he has missed. We learn from
Paddy that Charles Leavy, who is not there, appears to
stay up all night all the time. Paddy realises, to his
surprise, that he wants to be with Sinbad rather than
his friends.

Arriving home, Paddy resolves to be nice to his brother,
and realises that he has to prepare him for the
inevitable when his parents split up. He reflects that
the misleading thing about his home life is that his
mother's cooking remains as good as ever. Paddy again
attempts to look after Sinbad in an uncharacteristic way
by offering him milk. He tells his mother that he
appreciates his dinner very much.

Studying his father's mannerisms, Paddy realises that
he has come home drunk. When he tests his son's
spellings Mr Clarke gets two of them wrong, and
speaks in an unusual way. Paddy feels torn between his
mother and his father, and is unable to apportion blame
to either. He relates the fact that three other local
families have had their parents split up, and says that
he knows that the Clarkes are going to be next and
that he must be prepared.

Paddy watches Seán Whelan and Charles Leavy playing
football. He has seemingly given up writing his name in
cement, as he is sick of it. Kevin and Paddy try to join

in the game but are dismissed by the two new boys. By persisting they get involved in a game with Seán and Charles, only to be shouted at by Mrs Whelan, whose gate is the goal.

Paddy becomes fascinated by the harder and tougher of the two new boys, Charles Leavy. His bad language, tough manner, physical violence and don't-care attitude are all interesting to Paddy, who neglects Kevin in favour of Charles. One day he asks for a puff of his cigarette, and is amazed when Charles hands it to him. He is almost sickened by the strong cigarette, one of the strongest brands available, and tries desperately to pretend that he has enjoyed it. Charles tells him that he is trying to give them up.

While cultivating Charles's friendship and neglecting Kevin, Paddy is secretly making plans to run away, plotting to get the right supplies. He agonises again over the cause of his parents' arguments and asks himself why it is happening, finding himself unable to take sides. He does, however, reflect on how lovely his mother is and how superior she seems to the mothers of most of his friends, and wonders again why his father does not appreciate her. But though he thinks his father is more to blame than his mother, he still loves him because he is his father, and is torn between them. One night he goes to bed just after Sinbad, before he has to, and becomes very frightened, feeling like the younger brother rather than the elder. On the way to school the next morning he tries to make Sinbad understand how bad things are between their parents, but Sinbad does not want to listen.

In Mr Hennessey's class Paddy compares his strictness with the leniency of Miss Watkins, their previous teacher. He realises that Mr Hennessey's way is better, because more real learning takes place.

That night Mr Clarke does not come home, and Paddy
tries to cheer up his mother before he goes to bed. He
imagines, lying in bed, that his father dies and he is at
his funeral, but realises that this is just imagining. The
next day he decides to play truant from school,
following Charles Leavy away from the playground.
They talk about running away, and Charles seems to
know that Paddy is thinking of this course of action.
He stays at the edge of the school field for a while but
it is no fun, and he considers running away in order to
reunite his parents, but doubts that it will work.

Coming back into school after giving up the idea of
playing truant for the day, Paddy gets into an argument
with Kevin, who waits for him at break expecting a
fight. Paddy hurts his feelings by commenting on the
fact that at the medical inspection he saw Kevin's dirty
underwear. Kevin reacts with fury and there is a vicious
fight between him and Paddy, which Paddy narrowly
wins. He realises that things between him and his
former friend will never be the same again.

Kevin is still the most powerful influence over the other
boys, and he persuades them all to boycott Paddy.
When Paddy gets home his father is there and the
conversation seems relatively normal. His mother is

concerned at the state of his face and clothes, but seems glad that he won the fight when he tells her a little about it. Paddy decides that he is nearly ready to run away.

He misses conversation with the other boys at school but puts a brave face on being boycotted, deciding that the others can only boycott him if he does not want them to do so. All the same, it hurts him when even David Geraghty swings his crutch at him in the playground, saying that he was told to do so by Kevin. The other boys follow Kevin unanimously.

Paddy never gets the chance to run away. Before he carries out his plan, his father leaves home, not even taking a suitcase with him. Paddy knows that his mother will tell him solemnly that he is the man of the house now. In the playground the other boys taunt him with the rhyme:

> Paddy Clarke –
> Paddy Clarke –
> Has no da.
> Ha ha ha!

But Paddy realises suddenly that they no longer have any power to hurt him; they are 'only kids', and he has had to grow up suddenly.

The day before Christmas Eve Mr Clarke comes home for a visit, and has become a relative stranger to Paddy. He asks him how he is and shakes his hand as if he were already a man. Paddy replies formally. The growing-up process is complete.

COMMENT    In this section the problems between Mr and Mrs Clarke force themselves on Paddy and then on Sinbad, until Paddy plans to run away because he is unable to cope. The carefree accounts of games and gang activities are over, superseded by a desperate attempt on

Paddy's part to prevent the rows and to rationalise them. When Mr Hennessey brings Sinbad to him, with his tear-stained exercise book, Paddy suddenly realises that his brother is also being affected by the situation at home, and the two close ranks as Paddy promises Sinbad that he will not tell their mother what has happened despite Mr Hennessey's request that he does so. Paddy begins to feel close to his little brother and to show a preference for his company in a way which would have been alien to him at the beginning of the novel. When Paddy himself falls asleep in class, after he has stayed awake all night to prevent a fight at home, he wants only to be with Sinbad even though he has the interested sympathy of all his own classmates, and this realisation comes as a surprise to him.

*Paddy realises he is not alone in his suffering.*

The morning that his mother does not get up is frightening to Paddy not only because it is a change in his routine but also because he worries what it may portend for the future – a comparison is drawn in the reader's mind with Liam and Aidan's father, who does not get proper meals for his sons and allows them to do as they please. The crisp sandwiches that Paddy and Sinbad end up having because Paddy and his father are too inept to make proper sandwiches are a **symbol** (see Literary Terms) of this. When Paddy falls asleep in class, he has almost become like Liam, one of the boys who needs looking after by the teachers because of his home problems, and Mr Hennessey and the headmaster now treat Paddy with the same gentleness and tolerance that they have reserved for Liam and others like him. Paddy is anxious, when Mr Hennessey asks him if everything is all right at home, just to escape to his friends.

*Why do you think Paddy lies to Mr Hennessey about how things are at home?*

Paddy's friendship patterns change in this last section of the book. While life was normal at home, he felt secure, together with Kevin, looking down slightly on the life that Liam and Aidan lead with their father, with erratic meals, occasional days missed from school, and a general lack of routine and discipline. When things go wrong in the Clarke household he suddenly seems to realise that his family may become like Liam and Aidan's and seeks the company of Charles Leavy, who begins to fascinate him. Charles is in many ways beyond the experience of Paddy and his friends. His home life is plainly as dysfunctional as Liam and Aidan's but he is much tougher and his misdemeanours are much more hard and real than those of the gang, which mainly fall into the category of boyish mischief. When Paddy and Kevin try to play football with Charles and Seán, and Charles tells them to 'fuck off', Paddy realises that this is someone who is not afraid of Kevin the way the rest of the boys are. He also realises that he is secretly relieved when Kevin is sent home early for his grandmother's funeral, and he speaks to Liam in a much kinder way than he would have felt obliged to in order to stay on the right side of Kevin.

*Paddy's attitude to Sinbad has changed.*

Paddy's relationship with Sinbad also undergoes a change in this section. From being the little brother who is on the receiving end of Chinese burns and other torments, and who has to be 'managed' in front of his older friends, Sinbad becomes someone who Paddy sees as a person in his own right and Paddy's attitude to him becomes both protective and affectionate. He realises that he likes him and wants to be with him, and also that he can simply be himself with Sinbad without having to put on a front as he does with Kevin. Sinbad does not seem entirely happy or comfortable with this change, however. He sometimes withdraws from Paddy or does not talk to him – perhaps the changing relationship is too threatening for him.

Kevin becomes a problem to Paddy. Paddy asks him, in a desperate hope for reassurance, whether or not his parents ever fight, then realises firstly that Kevin is likely to use the information against him and secondly that what he has said may get back to his family. The realisation that Kevin uses information against people is a sudden one. Up to this point in the novel Paddy has happily and unthinkingly joined in with the teasing of Liam and Aidan about their irregular family life, and accepted it when Kevin has suddenly and temporarily decided that they are not part of the gang. Now, however, Paddy is vulnerable, and so he falls out with Kevin and seeks the friendship of the much tougher Charles Leavy, who never really associates with the other boys in the class.

*The atmosphere (see Literary Terms) of the story has become darker.*

The last thirty pages or so of the book are poignantly sad and show Paddy almost on a self-destructive course. His world is about to change forever and there is an awful inevitability about what happens as the story rushes to its conclusion. One minute he is resolving to help Sinbad 'get ready' for the end of their parents' marriage, the next he is telling himself that his mother's cooking never gets any worse, so surely nothing bad can be about to happen (p. 211). He spends most of the time watching one or other of his parents intently, trying desperately to work out why things have gone wrong, and struggling to come to terms with adult emotions. His childish vocabulary – for example, 'She was lovely. He was nice' (p. 213) – serves to emphasise how he is a child struggling to understand an adult conflict and has not the concepts to do so.

Paddy begins to study Charles Leavy closely, and seeks out his company more. The way in which the other boys conform begins to seem irrelevant to him, though at the same time he realises that Mr Hennessey's strictness is infinitely preferable to the leniency of Miss Watkins. There is an account of a lesson where Mr Hennessey checks the homework, and a comparison with Miss Watkins's methods, which is really the last good-humoured passage in the book. The settled and disciplined order of Mr Hennessey's class, with his gentle humour, is the last order left in Paddy's life.

Back at home, Paddy realises that his father's side of the bed has not been slept in and that he has stayed out all night. Almost as a direct reaction to this he follows Charles Leavy, who clearly does not want the company, off the school premises. When he asks Charles if he has ever run away, the other boy realises that Paddy is thinking of doing so, and all of a sudden Paddy feels stupid and decides to return to school.

Returning to school in time to join the line of boys waiting to go in, Paddy is kneed by Kevin, and instead of reacting as he usually does and taking it as a joke, he finds he really wants to hurt Kevin in return. His reaction is a mixture of irritation at Kevin for the trivial nature of his messing about when Paddy has such a lot on his mind, and anger at being his victim yet again.

*Paddy and Kevin's relationship is now one of bitterness.*

The viciousness of his retaliation as he kicks Kevin provokes Kevin into wanting a proper fight with him. Paddy suddenly realises that Kevin is not a real friend to him, and it is this above all which provokes the fight between them. Paddy gets the better of Kevin physically, then has to suffer a boycott by the rest of the class who follow Kevin's lead, as usual. All except Charles Leavy, who does not care.

*Things have changed forever.*

On p. 239 Paddy says 'It would never go back to the same again', and there is a feeling that his childhood ends at this moment. He displays a cold maturity in the way he reacts to the boycott: although he is hurt and misses talking to people he refuses to give the boys the satisfaction of knowing that he is worried, even when David Geraghty unexpectedly whips him with his crutches, an act which seems to upset David as much as

Paddy. He has probably done it only because he is afraid of Kevin's actions if he refuses.

Abruptly, Paddy's rambling and lively accounts of his life come to an end with his father's departure. To his surprise, he tries to cry and cannot. He sits there in shock, having seen his father hit his mother again then leave, closing the front door behind him, then waits for his mother to explain to him that he is the man of the house now, because 'That was the way it always happened' (p. 246). There is a terrible weariness in the way he relates this, and also in the way he dismisses the boys at school when they make up a rhyme about Paddy having 'no da'.

The final paragraph continues in the same flat, guarded tone with an account of his father's visit just before Christmas, which conveys the new distance between the two, and also the distance between the Paddy Clarke of the rest of the novel and the one who has had to grow up overnight.

GLOSSARY      **Richard Nixon** (1913–94) former American senator, elected President of the USA in 1968

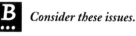

### A  *Identify the speaker.*

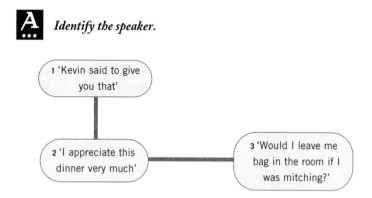

1 'Kevin said to give you that'

2 'I appreciate this dinner very much'

3 'Would I leave me bag in the room if I was mitching?'

*Identify the person 'to whom' this comment refers.*

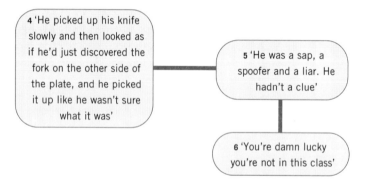

4 'He picked up his knife slowly and then looked as if he'd just discovered the fork on the other side of the plate, and he picked it up like he wasn't sure what it was'

5 'He was a sap, a spoofer and a liar. He hadn't a clue'

6 'You're damn lucky you're not in this class'

Check your answers on page 95.

### B  *Consider these issues.*

a  Why Paddy becomes fascinated by Charles Leavy.

b  Why the fight breaks out between Paddy and Kevin and how their relationship changes in this part of the book.

c  Whether Paddy really wants his family life to be like Liam and Aidan's, as he sometimes seems to.

d  How the style (see Literary Terms) and language of the story change in this last section as Paddy's family life deteriorates.

# PART THREE

# COMMENTARY

## THEMES

*Paddy Clarke Ha Ha Ha* is essentially a 'rites of passage' novel, or '*Bildungsroman*' (see Literary Terms), about a boy growing into a young man. It deals with this main theme through the context of an Irish Catholic upbringing and dwells particularly on two other themes: that of the delightful humour and innate cruelty of small boys towards each other; and the less light-hearted theme of family breakdown which gradually emerges, and comes to dominate the latter part of the book.

### RITES OF PASSAGE

The novel is a first-person account of Paddy Clarke's life, down to the last detail of what he has for tea, told as though the narrator (see Literary Terms) is actually ten years old. Until the last section of the book, indeed until the last few pages, the reader is made to feel that the events in the novel happen entirely in the present (see also Structure and Language & Style). There are certain set pieces (see Literary Terms) in the accounts of games, the activities of the gang and the lessons at school which are typical of novels about growing up, for example the football match, Grand National and the swear word game. What makes these events particularly vivid is their immediacy and the level of detail included in the telling – the enormous excitement and vitality in Paddy's accounts of such incidents transport the reader back to his or her own childhood.

Paddy's place in the family as the eldest child is important to the process of his growing up. At first he hates his younger brother and treats him in the way expected of older brothers. Sinbad is the target of dead legs and Chinese burns, has soap suds flicked in his eyes, is force-fed a Swiss roll and is shut in a large suitcase. He even has lighter fuel put in his mouth and set on fire. Paddy is also proud of being the eldest: when he dusts the family picture in his parents' bedroom on Sundays there is a sense of tradition and continuity, and he is excited at the prospect of being as tall as his father. Through his friendship with Kevin he is aware of the alternative advantages and disadvantages of being the younger brother, one of which is the fact that you are allowed into the house with the Scalextric!

*Paddy begins to treat Sinbad more kindly.*

As Paddy becomes more aware of the situation between his parents he develops a more sentimental approach to Sinbad, deciding that he likes him and that it is his duty to prepare him for, and to some extent protect him from, what is about to happen to their family.

Paddy's innocence (as well as that of his friends) is displayed in the earlier parts of the novel in many ways: in his touching desire to be like Father Damien, working with the lepers; in his belief that George Best has personally signed his football book; and in his naïve fear that he will die from a jellyfish sting because Edward Swanwick tells him so. His accounts of the various scrapes the gang gets into are underpinned by the belief that the worst thing in life which can happen is that you get caught and 'killed', i.e. chastised, or at worst hit by a parent or teacher. He and Kevin even consider, on the first page, that it would be 'brilliant' to have a dead mother, thinking only of the special treatment Liam seems to get from teachers, and never considering the real implications.

In the later parts of the novel, however, Paddy's innocence is tempered by his growing awareness of the family conflict and the impending break-up of his parents' marriage. The bewilderment he feels is

conveyed vividly when he wonders why his father no
longer loves his mother, and above all in the heart-
stopping moment when he first hears a smack. The
relationships between the gang members become
darker too, with Paddy beginning to realise – and
resent – the extent to which Kevin dominates the
others, and adjusting his treatment of Liam and Aidan
when Kevin is not there. At the end of the novel, as
Mr and Mrs Clarke are breaking up, there is a parallel
divorce of Paddy from his friends as he falls out with
Kevin and becomes fascinated with Charles Leavy –
who is already experienced in ways of family breakdown
unknown to the gang.

### THE IRISH CATHOLIC BACKGROUND

Catholicism forms a backdrop to the novel which helps
to explain the boy Paddy is and the young man he
becomes by the end (see also Context & Setting). It is a
part of Paddy's family life, so much so that it is taken
for granted, and thus it is all the more shocking to
Paddy when his family life does not live up to the
Christian ideals described in the religious teaching he
has received. The Clarke family is a practising one;
references are made to Paddy helping with the
housework before Sunday Mass, and to the breakfast
being finished in time to allow the family to fast for the
required duration before receiving Communion (after

*Mr Clarke does*
*not seem to take*
*his faith as*
*seriously as his*
*wife does.*

the Second Vatican Council in 1962 this duration was
set at one hour). It is obvious that Paddy's mother is
more devout than his father. When Paddy says he has a
vocation to the priesthood Mrs Clarke is pleased,
though his father seems annoyed and appears to feel
that someone, maybe his wife, has been indoctrinating
Paddy and that the idea of being a priest is not his own.
Mr Clarke also, as Paddy notices one Sunday after his
parents have had a row, fails to observe the required fast

by finishing his breakfast less than one hour before
Mass. If, as it seems, Mr Clarke begins the chain of
events leading to the family break-up, he is perhaps
more guilty about failing to live up to the teachings of
the Church and therefore more inclined to make light
of those teachings.

At school the religious background is also significant.
The Faith is taught by the teachers and by Father
Moloney, the parish priest, and lessons include the lives
of saints and holy priests such as Father Damien, who
inspires Paddy to play his lepers game.

Among the lessons learned by Paddy are warnings
about what happens to sinners, and in his innocence he
takes much of the Church teaching literally, really
believing that he will go to Purgatory for stealing, and
that there is a tariff according to which stealing *Football
Monthly* carries the highest penalty of four million
years. This literal acceptance, typical of young children,
is also shown in Paddy's innocent and touching
concern for his stillborn sister, as he wonders whether
the water of baptism touched her before she died,
because otherwise she will end up in Limbo. Paddy has
a well-developed conscience about wrongdoing, and
though mischievous in the extreme, is actually worried
about his parents, teachers and the priest thinking badly
of him. We also see that he is worried about
wrongdoing itself, for example when he is so terrified of
his mother having seen him stealing the copies of
*Woman's Way* in Raheny, or when he is afraid that Mrs
Kiernan will somehow read his mind and discover what
the gang have done to her knickers.

### HUMOUR AND REALISM

Roddy Doyle effectively conveys exactly what boys are
like, particularly in gangs and when they are not with

their parents. All of the elements typical of boys' gangs are there: the endless dead legs and Chinese burns, the ridiculous jokes, the fascination with snot and excrement. We laugh with Paddy at the various 'brilliant' experiences of the gang: setting fire to a rat, stuffing a dead guinea-pig through a letter box, writing their names in cement, and trapping bees in tarmac. The gang mentality – milling around in packs, on their bikes, playing in the building sites – is **realistically** (see Literary Terms) presented, for example in the incident when they have to go back for Paddy's jumper left on a building site and they are listening out for the watchman: in the few words 'We heard something; Kevin did' (p. 7) the nervousness of the boys and the togetherness of the gang are conveyed.

*There is a serious side to many of the humorous incidents.*

There are many light-hearted moments in the book, but even those we laugh at are threaded through with unease. We may be amused by the boys' fear of the medical inspection, but we are left in no doubt as to how real and serious it feels to them. Even the swear word game, funny as it is, has disturbing undertones when Liam refuses to play because he will not be hit with the poker any longer, and becomes a temporary outcast. Indeed, the way in which Kevin, often supported by the others, outlaws Liam and Aidan when he feels like it, just because their mother is dead and their home life is not as regular as that of the others, is frightening at times.

Generally the boys play and slap one another around harmlessly (while the adults' conflict is far from harmless) but there are also more sinister moments such as when Paddy fights Seán Whelan, Charles Leavy kicks him, and he suddenly realises that no-one is going to 'jump in' and support him. Everyone is quiet, looking on, and the pack mentality, the savagery that is never far below the surface, emerges clearly.

## FAMILY BREAKDOWN

*Paddy Clarke Ha Ha Ha* is in many ways a very funny book, and much of the humour and warmth of Paddy's life in 1960s Ireland comes through, but the novel is also an extremely sad story of a family in crisis. Paddy's gradual realisation that his parents are going to split up is shared, poignantly and vividly and without sentimentality, with the reader. By the last page, Paddy may have suppressed his tears and become the man of the house, but the reader finds it easy to cry for him. At the start of the novel, we are given a warm and comforting picture of a kindly and sensible mother who doesn't fuss unnecessarily over her sons but is there for them when needed, and loves all of her children. Paddy's father teaches him tricks, listens to his spellings and shares jokes with him. The house is clean and well cared for, delicious meals are on the table at regular intervals, and family life is ordered, good-humoured and full of easy warmth.

*Paddy appreciates the regularity of his home life.*

By way of contrast, Paddy takes a sideways look at the families of some of his friends. Liam and Aidan's family is the most different compared to Paddy's own, with the mother dead, the father often drunk and not coping well with her loss, and the children being packed off to an aunt when he brings his girlfriend home. He does not run an ordered domestic life, bringing home take-away meals and allowing his children and their friends to play raucously on the furniture. Because of this, the two boys are sometimes the butt of jokes and are left out by Kevin and the other members of the gang.

When he compares his own mother with those of his friends later in the book, in a vain attempt to explain to himself why his father has ceased to love her, Paddy finds all the mothers wanting in some way. Even Kevin, whose family seems fairly similar to the Clarkes, has an older brother who has been in more trouble than the Clarkes have heard of, while Ian McEvoy's mother is 'horrible', as are Charles Leavy's and Seán Whelan's. James O'Keefe's mother arrives at school to berate Mr Hennessey for picking on her son, to his embarrassment, while Edward Swanwick's mother mollycoddles him. Paddy is all the more shocked, therefore, when his 'normal' family life breaks down and he becomes like Liam and Aidan. This change is reflected in certain aspects of the novel's structure: Liam and Aidan have crisp sandwiches for lunch, which Paddy envies while his mother is making him cheese and ham ones; then comes the day when Mrs Clarke fails to get up and Mr Clarke gives Paddy money for crisp sandwiches. At the beginning of the novel Mr Hennessey and the headmaster are kind to Liam when he dirties his trousers, because of his background; by the end, the same two teachers show the same kindness to Paddy when he falls asleep in class because he has stayed up all night trying to prevent a fight between his parents.

*Paddy's teachers are sympathetic to his changed circumstances.*

Towards the end of the book Paddy becomes increasingly aware of the impending break-up, to the extent that he breaks up with his friends, unable perhaps to relate to them now his circumstances have changed so much, and prepares to run away. Before he can do so, however, his father leaves home and he is abruptly catapulted into manhood. His first impulse when his father walks out is to howl, but he suppresses it and hides his anguish. He expects his mother to call him over and tell him that he is the man of the house now, and at school the disrespectful rhymes, chanted by the gang earlier about other people, are now aimed at him. However, in the sentence 'They were only kids' he dismisses them together with his childhood and all it has stood for.

The final terse paragraph shows a boy who has had to
grow up prematurely, greeting his father on his
Christmas visit in a manner which is frighteningly
controlled and almost cold. We want to weep for the
loss of Paddy's father, and his childhood, and his
innocence.

# STRUCTURE

In many ways the structure of this novel breaks many
rules: rather than following a strict chronological order
and having a distinct plot, *Paddy Clarke Ha Ha Ha* is
chaotic, **episodic** and full of unfinished descriptions and
**non sequiturs** (see Literary Terms) which are typical of
childhood experience. In these respects the structure
accurately reflects the subject matter and themes of the
story.

There is a sense of timelessness to the way the book is
structured (see also Language & Style): the **narrative**
(see Literary Terms) is constructed as though Paddy is
currently ten years old, has always – except for one brief
**flashback** (see Literary Terms) – been ten years old,
and – until the final few pages of the book – will always
be ten years old.

In the space of one page, Paddy, who narrates
throughout, may dwell on the smell of a hot water
bottle, the anxiety he feels at hearing his parents
arguing, a conversation between him and the gang, an
earlier memory of his father, and an incident at school,
all in no particular order. The more memorable
incidents such as the great Barrytown United football
match and the swear word game get more space
devoted exclusively to them, but even then they are
often interspersed with little asides about home life, the
meanings of words, the lifespan of animals or other

interesting facts or observations which Paddy suddenly remembers. Sometimes these are even in the middle of sentences.

The first part of the book provides us with an unsorted stream of games, mischief and gang get-togethers, interspersed with incidents at school and at home. All are narrated with breathless pace and some humour, and even when it seems that the boys may get into *Paddy's anxiety* trouble, there is a sense that nothing very bad will *gradually intrudes* happen. As the story progresses, however, the reader *into the structure.* becomes aware of Paddy's increasing uneasiness at home, at first in mid-sentence or mid-paragraph interruptions, then as the accounts of fights and tension in the family gradually take over longer sections of the **narrative** (see Literary Terms).

In the middle of the novel we find the only sustained **flashback** (see Literary Terms), of the fort Paddy had under the dining room table when he was a very young boy. This serves to demarcate the carefree first section from the rest of the **narrative** (see Literary Terms) where there is increasing tension. The conflict features more prominently in the story right up to the last few pages, which present a stark, sparse account of the end of Paddy's childhood and normal family life.

Running alongside the build-up to his parents' split is the separation of Paddy from his gang, and particularly from his friendship with Kevin. Paddy is seen to be a safe member of the gang at the beginning; dominated by Kevin as they all are, but safely on the inside when Liam and Aidan are sometimes despised or made outcasts. The entrance of the Corporation boys Seán and Charles disturbs the balance of relationships in the gang, but it is the situation at home which (at least partially) motivates Paddy's fascination with Charles, who obviously comes from a dysfunctional family. At the end of the book Paddy seems determined to sever the links he has had with Kevin, and the fight between them – the culmination of this process – is deliberately started by Paddy. The divorce from his friends, when Kevin demands a 'boycott', in many ways parallels the divorce at home (see also Themes).

The seemingly illogical structure of Paddy's **narrative** (see Literary Terms), often jumping abruptly from one idea to another, effectively conveys the mixture of fascination, exuberance and bewilderment with which he approaches life as it unfolds during the novel. There is a deliberate lack of **authorial comment**, which ensures that the story is told as **realistically** as possible from Paddy's **viewpoint** (see Literary Terms).

# CHARACTERS

## PADDY CLARKE

Paddy is exuberant, energetic and enthusiastic. He is interested in everything and collects facts, which he introduces into his **narrative** (see Literary Terms) at any suitable or unsuitable moment as he thinks of them. He plays around in class enough to avoid the peer group pressure which might lead to being called a 'swot' but is clearly intelligent and quick-witted, often with an answer for everything, though not as ready-witted as his friend Kevin.

*Energetic*
*Bright*
*Mischievous*
*Enquiring*

Paddy is full of mischief; he thinks it funny to write his name in wet cement and commit other acts of vandalism. Adults who might interfere with his childish pleasures are dismissed as witches or evil, and the watchman and the Hanleys are considered fair game for tormenting. His fascination for facts is equalled by that for snot, excrement and the sticky stuff that you wake up with in your eyes; this fascination is typical of young boys and in Paddy's case is an extension of his hunger for life and experience. He is passionate about his enthusiasms for football, The Three Stooges and Geronimo. He is also naïve and has an innocent desire to do good – he wants to be like Father Damien and help the lepers – and his imagination is highly developed – he imagines himself being a footballer or a missionary with equal ease. He is sufficiently worldly-wise to recognise that Kevin is the dominant one in the gang and in their friendship, and he seems not to resent this, though he is aware of it, until the end of the novel. By then he has become aware of his parents' conflict and also of the way in which Kevin treats Liam and Aidan as inferior because of their family situation, and he knows that Kevin will inevitably behave in a similar way towards him. This precipitates the break-up of their friendship.

Paddy's innocence is shown in the gradual revelation of his parents' marital breakdown and its effect on him. He is helpless and bewildered in the face of matters beyond his control. Emotions are close to the surface and inextricably tangled; love and hate, fear and pleasure. He is acutely sensitive, but unable to explain the discord at home. He is an affectionate child who cannot understand why the father and mother he loves cannot love each other any more, or why his safe and comfortable world is about to come crashing down on his shoulders.

MR CLARKE
*Humorous*
*Hard-working*
*Eccentric*
*Interested in*
*world affairs*

At the beginning of the novel Mr Clarke is a gentle, humorous and supportive father, who tells his sons jokes, listens to their reading and spelling and treats his family with slightly distant but warm affection. Paddy sometimes finds him slightly intimidating, especially as he does not like to be disturbed when he is watching the news on television or reading the newspapers. He takes a keen interest in Irish and world politics and is

quick to comment on the behaviour of politicians with some cynicism. He treats the media cynically too, for example when he tells Paddy not to worry about the headlines generated by the Arab–Israeli conflict and that there is unlikely to be a World War Three. He is something of an idealist, as revealed when he talks to Paddy about his secret wish to live in Israel, which he believes is based, as a new country, on an ideal society. He is sometimes eccentric and funny, bringing home old records, teaching his sons to sing, and playing games with them. He is genuinely interested in and supportive of their education and takes time to explain things, in particular to Paddy. We also know that he is quite strict – Paddy tells us that his father does not wear a belt, but keeps one for the purpose of punishment. He seems to be more interested in his sons than in his daughters, perhaps because they are very young and he does not know how to treat babies and toddlers, but we sense that he is more at home in male company than female.

Mr Clarke's idealism is soured by what is happening in his family life. As more children have been born his wife seems to have become more preoccupied with the little ones and the couple seem to him to have drifted apart; perhaps this is why he discusses world affairs with Paddy rather than with Mrs Clarke. He tries to please his wife, buying a car and taking her out, but somehow whatever he does is no longer good enough and they drift still further apart. He seems angry and bewildered by this at different times, and takes an increasingly aggressive attitude towards his wife as the story progresses. Towards the end he gets drunk in order to forget his troubles and comes home in the evenings spoiling for a fight.

His attitude to his religion becomes more ambivalent as his marriage deteriorates. When, after the Father

Damien game, Paddy tells his mother that he has a
vocation, Mr Clarke accuses his wife of indoctrinating
the boy and clearly is not altogether pleased at the idea
of Paddy becoming a priest. He seems to feel that his
faith has been a disappointment.

MRS CLARKE　Mrs Clarke is gentle and affectionate. She loves all of
her children dearly but is not over-possessive of her
sons, allowing Paddy a certain measure of independence
as he gets older. She treats him with a matter-of-fact
tenderness: for example, when he thinks a jellyfish has
stung him she does not fuss in an over-protective
manner but offers ointment and a cuddle, as soon as she
has finished feeding her two young daughters. She is
patient and tender with Paddy and Sinbad, calming
night fears and explaining things which puzzle them.

*Gentle*
*Loving*
*Strict*
*Preoccupied with*
*her family*

She is a good housekeeper who, without making a great
fuss about it, keeps the home spotless, and provides
regular nourishing and delicious meals even when her
marriage is breaking down around her. (One of the
reasons Paddy tells himself that things will be all right
between his parents after all is because his mother's
dinners never cease to be delicious.) Her attitude to
world affairs and to her faith is simpler than Mr
Clarke's and she is delighted when Paddy talks about a
vocation; it does not occur to her that her husband
would not be so happy. She seems to be an intelligent
woman, however, and reads widely. We get the
impression that she has submerged her wider interests
for the time being to bring up her family.

Although she is gentle with her sons she is a strict
parent who brings them up to respect God, their elders
and the Church. Paddy, partly because of her strictness
and partly because of his love for her, is utterly terrified
when she sees them stealing women's magazines in
Raheny. Because she has done her duty lovingly, being
a good wife and mother, she seems as bewildered as her

husband when things go wrong between them. Perhaps she has spent so much time home-making and being absorbed in the children that she has lost touch with him as a man and a partner. Paddy clearly adores her and sees little wrong with her except that she is 'too busy'; but what woman with four children would not be?

## KEVIN

*Funny*
*Daring*
*Cruel*
*Mischievous*
*A leader*

Kevin is very much the gang leader, harder and tougher than Paddy, and both looked up to and envied at times by him. It is always Kevin who decides what the gang will play, and thinks of more daring things to do (to steal the biggest box from the shops, for example). He is the judge in Voyage To The Bottom Of The Sea, the high priest in the swear word game, and the one who decides which footballer they will all be before they play a match. Because he has an older brother, he has more ideas (gleaned from him) about interesting games. He is more daring because he follows his brother's bad example, and he sometimes gains privileges like being admitted to the older boys' houses to see their new toys, though as a little brother he is still not allowed to play with the Scalextric, only to watch.

Kevin has a distinctly cruel streak which Paddy often observes. The boys are all cruel and affectionate by turns, expressing their friendships in terms of dead legs, Chinese burns and insults, but Kevin takes it a bit further, often deciding who is in and who is out of the gang. He is particularly cruel to Liam and Aidan, sometimes deciding that they are not allowed to play, and physically as well as emotionally tormenting the younger Aidan by attempting to bury him in mud. Kevin is always the first to make rude and suggestive remarks about adults and older children.

So why does Paddy follow him, and why is he popular? He is fun, with a cruel but sharp wit, and a keen sense of enjoyment. He is attractive, strong and a good footballer. His daring attracts the other boys because they enjoy seeing him do things which they don't quite dare do, and his sarcastic and rude remarks make them laugh. He is always prepared to go one step further than anyone else and that makes him something of a hero. There is also the element of insecurity Kevin engenders in the other boys; they stay loyal to him out of fear, because if you are with Kevin you are not on the outside. Only Liam, already outcast by virtue of his family situation, dares to defy Kevin; when he leaves the camp fire Paddy reflects that it is better to be hit with the poker by Kevin the high priest than to go where Liam is going. It is only when Paddy's senses are sharpened by his awareness of the conflict at home that he becomes aware of the injustice in Kevin's treatment of him and the others, and wishes to break the friendship with him.

SINBAD

*Placid*
*Tolerant*
*Nervous*
*Cries easily*

Paddy's younger brother, real name Francis, at first seems to be there to be tormented. He is a 'great crier' who Paddy has to protect and manage. When Sinbad gets stuck in a hedge while the gang are running away from the watchman on the building site, Paddy is obliged to go back for him even at the risk of getting caught. He receives more dead legs and Chinese burns than all the rest of the boys put together, and is subjected to having lighter fuel poured into his mouth and his lips set on fire. Paddy is furious and worried because he cannot 'sort out' Sinbad in this incident.

Sinbad is more protected than Paddy, and in material terms treated less well, receiving smaller birthday presents and less pocket money. He seems babyish to Paddy, yet during a football match Paddy is made to realise that Sinbad is a natural player, with, as Mr O'Keefe says, the 'perfect centre of gravity' for a footballer. He throws himself into the game with energy and commitment, unlike most of the older

boys, who play just for fun and never run towards
the ball. He is patient and endures whatever torment
Paddy dishes out, seeming to accept it pacifically as a
younger brother's lot. He is more nervous of adults
and of getting caught out in wrongdoing than Paddy
is.

Towards the end of the novel Paddy's attitude to
Sinbad changes. Sinbad has grown beyond babyhood
and Paddy realises that he likes him for his placid
nature, his tolerance of being the younger brother and
his being there and being able to talk to him on more
equal terms. Sinbad is not altogether comfortable with
this change, and seems almost threatened by it.

### LIAM & AIDAN

Liam and Aidan's mother is dead and their father is
often drunk and has a girlfriend, behaviour which is
disapproved of by the local community. His house is
not especially clean, meals are irregular and often from
the take-away, and he allows the local children to play
boisterously on the furniture. All of these things make
Liam different, as well as the fact that he is treated
sympathetically by the teachers at school. Kevin is quick
to pick on this and the others join in. While Paddy
likes him and enjoys his friendship, Paddy is always
wary of the fact that Kevin sometimes rejects him
because of his more disadvantaged family background,
and never dares to be as close to him as perhaps he
would like.

Liam clearly remembers his mother better than his
younger brother Aidan does, and he misses her. He is
not communicative – when asked about missing her he
just 'breathed' (p. 33); he has suppressed a lot of his
sorrow. He clearly resents Margaret, his father's new
girlfriend, for trying to take his mother's place. His

response to the teasing by the others is usually silence, but he does speak out on the occasion of the swear word game when he refuses to be dominated by Kevin. This takes a certain courage, but in Liam's case it is the courage of desperation. He does express what they all feel, though, and perhaps because of his actions they all refuse to play the following Friday because they are sick of being hit with the poker.

*Paddy likes Liam, even though Paddy is often cruel to him.*

Liam is not as bright as Kevin or Paddy, and while they are both aware of this it is Kevin who takes advantage, verbally putting Liam down at every opportunity, and getting him to light the fuel in Sinbad's mouth in case they get caught. Liam is a follower rather than a leader. Paddy is not sure why he likes him, maybe because he is unassuming and content to follow, but he is sure that he does. When Kevin is not there he treats Liam as an equal, but when Kevin is present it is a different story and Paddy can be as cruel as Kevin. He acknowledges this when Kevin is visiting his grandmother (p. 190). Despite the fact that Liam seems unassuming, he has a dangerous streak in him, which Paddy recognises when he considers fighting him; Liam would have won.

Often treated the same as his elder brother Liam, Aidan is also affected by his mother's death. Like Sinbad, he is a good footballer, although the older boys do not recognise this at first. He displays unexpected humour and wit in his commentaries on the football matches and some of the gang's games, making Paddy realise that he is cleverer than they thought. Like Sinbad, Aidan is the victim of various torments, at one time being almost buried alive by the rest of the gang in a trench of wet earth. To some extent he is a younger echo of Liam, and Paddy portrays him as having something of the same dangerous quality if provoked.

## MINOR CHARACTERS

*Mr Hennessey*

Paddy's teacher is a strict disciplinarian of the type which was already becoming old-fashioned during the 1960s. 'Henno' is humorous, tolerant of the many failings of young boys, and always expects the best from them in terms of effort, good manners and neatness of presentation. He holds weekly tests after which he changes the boys' seating order to reflect the current order of merit, and expects the boys to take pride in doing their best at all times. He often cracks jokes using his own brand of eccentric humour and expects his pupils to laugh. His classroom repartee often consists of making fun of the boys' efforts in a good-humoured way.

Mr Hennessey seems to have eyes in the back of his head and can maintain discipline from afar, as he does if he has a visitor, or one of the boys is ill and needs attention, or a parent or medical inspection interferes with the classroom routine. He is thought by the parents to be a good teacher because he teaches the basics of reading, spelling and mental arithmetic and drills the boys thoroughly, tolerating no misbehaviour or lack of effort in his class. The only exception is James O'Keefe's mother, who insists that Hennessey picks on her son; indeed he does appear to dislike James in particular. When Liam dirties his trousers and Paddy falls asleep in class he shows himself to be tolerant and understanding, making allowances for personal problems the boys may be encountering. Paddy finds his sudden questioning about whether everything is all right at home intrusive and wants to go back to the old, more distant relationship he normally has with his teacher.

*Ian McEvoy*

Ian is another gang member who readily joins in the mischief, though he is not as daring as Paddy and

Kevin. He seems at times to be over-protected by his mother, and lashes out at this in the incident when his guinea-pig dies and he uses his sister's doll to make, with the gang, an effigy of his mother. Ian often seems unlucky, cutting his foot on booby traps and getting hit by Mr Hennessey when he falls asleep during the Friday spelling test.

*Charles Leavy*

One of the 'Corporation boys', Charles comes from a rougher background than Paddy, with a tough-looking mother, no father in evidence, a smoking habit he is trying to give up, and a nervous tic which Paddy describes as being like heading an imaginary ball. This perhaps represents Charles's aggressive attitude to life. When Paddy fights the other Corporation boy, Seán Whelan, Charles does not obey the usual childish codes of playground fighting but kicks Paddy from the side. He is so vicious that the others are all afraid of him, and do not include him in their mock fighting games, dead legs, Chinese burns or sly pokes in the ribs. Paddy develops a fascination with him towards the end of the novel which is clearly linked to the fact that Charles is somehow outside and beyond the boys' relatively innocent world. He seems years older in terms of streetwise experience.

*Seán Whelan*

The other boy from the Corporation houses is calmer and more ordinary than Charles, though he has some of the same aggression and is not afraid to stand up for himself. Both boys would be thought 'rough' by Paddy's parents, which is part of their attraction for Paddy, and Seán is also streetwise, swearing as a matter of course as Charles does, rather than using four-letter words to shock as the boys in the gang do.

*David Geraghty*

Having had polio when younger, David is on crutches, which makes him interesting to the other boys and yet places him outside the gang as he cannot join in their very physical games and mischief. Always near or at the top desk, he is the brightest boy in the class academically, and has a ready wit and sense of **irony** (see Literary Terms) which Paddy discovers when he is forced to sit next to him after a good performance in the tests. He is well liked despite being something of an outsider, and therefore the fact that he joins in Kevin's boycott with his crutches hurts Paddy all the more.

*James*
*O'Keefe*

James is on the fringes of the gang. A naughtier boy in class than Kevin or Paddy, he is frequently in trouble with Mr Hennessey, who appears to dislike him intensely, perhaps because of his lack of effort and commitment at school. James is often at the centre of the more outrageous behaviour; for example it is he who is caught 'pruning' a less able boy and invokes the wrath of the headmaster.

*Edward*
*Swanwick*

Edward is a spoilt boy who is over-protected by his mother. He is regarded as 'soft' by the other boys for this reason and also due to the fact that he attends a private school. Like the younger brothers, he is the butt of the older boys' jokes and is forced to swallow soap powder by the gang. At the end of the novel it is mentioned that his family have split up and that he has moved away, never to be seen by Paddy again.

*Miss Watkins*

Paddy's former class teacher is used to show how much less strict she was than Mr Hennessey. Paddy describes her methods of conducting the Friday test which allowed the more unscrupulous boys to cheat. When he claims that his grandfather was the Mr Clarke who signed the 1916 Proclamation of Independence, she is not fooled, however. Paddy makes it clear that he respects her less than he does Mr Hennessey.

*Mr*
*Finnucane*

The headmaster of the school is a fairly remote figure. Although strict like Mr Hennessey, his manner is mild and he seems to like the children in his care, as we see, for example, when he is distant but kind to Paddy on the day he falls asleep in class.

**Father Moloney**
The parish priest's regular Religious Education lessons inform Paddy's thinking about vocations, his admiration for Father Damien, his fear of going to Purgatory for stealing from shops and his dread that his stillborn younger sister had ended up in Limbo because the baptismal water failed to touch her before she died. Mrs Clarke respects him as the representative of the Church but Mr Clarke seems annoyed at some of the ideas Paddy gets from Father Moloney's teaching.

**Mr O'Connell**
Liam and Aidan's father is at first frequently drunk as he mourns his dead wife, then happier as he settles down with his girlfriend. He has a relaxed attitude to housekeeping, and does not appear to care what the neighbours may think of him.

**Margaret**
Mr O'Connell's new girlfriend tries hard to introduce some domesticity into the lives of the family and to treat the boys kindly and fairly, bringing them sweets and cooking good meals. Characteristically, Aidan, who remembers his mother less, accepts her, but Liam does not.

**Liam and Aidan's Aunt**
Liam and Aidan are frequently sent to their real aunt in Raheny, to avoid the 'scandal' of their father's relationship with his girlfriend. Their aunt is kind and domestic, with a life centred round her family, the community in Raheny and the news.

**Mrs Quigley**
An older neighbour, Mrs Quigley is ready to blame the gang for any damage done to her house, especially her windows. Paddy and his friends torment her by banging on her gate with sticks.

**The Kilmartins**
The Kilmartins are also older neighbours, and again the butt of the gang's practical jokes, this time the dead

|  | guinea-pig through the letter box and the knickers being headbutted in the garden. |
|---|---|
| *The Hanleys* | Owners of the garden at the end of the gang's 'Grand National' course, Mr Hanley and his two grown-up sons Billy and Laurence are justifiably angry when the boys regularly hurtle through their property. |
| *Luke (Fluke) Cassidy* | Remarkable at school for his epilepsy, Luke has a fit during the Friday cinema show, and is another member of the class on the fringes of Paddy's gang. |
| *Martin* | Kevin's older brother is even more daring than Kevin and has perhaps provided the example for some of the gang's worst exploits. |
| *Terence Long* | Martin's friend Terence is also much naughtier and more daring than Paddy's gang. |
| *Catherine and Deirdre* | Paddy's younger sisters barely feature in the story except when he becomes aware of them while he is talking to his mother as she feeds them. Catherine's asthma is blamed for the family not being able to have a pet. |
| *Shopkeepers* | Mr Fitzpatrick is generous; Tootsie is clearly somewhat simple; and the ladies who run the Raheny bakery and the newsagent's are wise to the ways of young boys and let them get away with very little. |
| *Other neighbours and parents* | The various other adults in Paddy's world, who we often only hear rumours or snippets of information about, provide a backdrop to the story. |

# LANGUAGE & STYLE

The effects of the novel are achieved by the language and style working hand-in-hand with the structure to create **realistically** (see Literary Terms) the world of a ten-year-old boy in 1960s Ireland. One of the ways in which the author gets into the mind of a ten-year-old is through the use of a series of very short simple sentences in a paragraph. The description of Paddy being taught to ride a bike by his father (p. 132) is a clear example of this. Another example is the description of the fort on pp. 90–1, where the short sentences and the simplicity of the style convey the idea of a much younger Paddy in what is the main **flashback** (see Literary Terms) of the novel. Sometimes these short sentences have a compression which conveys a sense of nervy anxiety, as when Paddy is forced to wait in his bedroom for punishment after Mrs Quigley's window is broken: 'I hated it; it worked' (p. 68).

The author's purpose is clearly to keep the sentences short and simple, suggesting the sort of writing you might find in a child's exercise book, but over 200 pages of this would probably be too much, so he also builds longer sentences, often using semicolons as punctuation, but lets them drift on until the **syntax** (see Literary Terms) collapses and the words still sound as though a junior school boy might have said them. An example of this is the description of the building sites at the beginning of the novel (p. 4) where a whole list of features is enumerated until the sentence barely holds together.

Chronologically, the **narrative** (see Literary Terms) often fails to hold together, with the childish questions and the complete **non sequiturs** (see Literary Terms) intruding in the middle of sentences. When Paddy begins to tell the story of Father Damien there is a sudden recalling of the fact that 'All the grown-ups drank dark Flemish beer' (p. 40), and the sort of questions boys ask each other in the playground often intrude in the middle of a paragraph, for example 'Are there any lepers in Ireland?' (p. 43).

The description of the Grand National game is a good example of how the style of narration reflects the patterns of a child's speech. In the middle of describing Liam's broken teeth comes a digression to explain the game itself, and then he returns to Liam's pain, before digressing again to Mrs Quigley and the time he and Kevin broke her window, with their childish speculations as to the reasons for the Quigleys having no children in the middle. Chaotic and illogical as it is, the style works because it is true to the patterns of childish thought and speech.

The vocabulary is generally simple and reflects the boyish obsessions with snot, excrement, swear words and sticky stuff, with childish rhymes and conjecturing about the sex lives of the neighbours, who they love to torment. Occasionally Paddy seems to have an unnaturally expanded vocabulary, though this is partly explained by the fact that he collects new words and facts and is a voracious reader. There are times when the words chosen to describe something perhaps seem too apt or precisely chosen to be the language of a boy, for example the use of the word 'rushed' (p. 1) to describe the smell which assailed the boys when Liam dirtied his trousers, but the author returns often to the words of boyhood (for example, the use of the words 'brilliant' and 'stupid' to describe virtually everything) in order to maintain a sense of **realism** (see Literary Terms). The narration reflects on tiny details like the smell or texture of things, but also creates the effect of a wider canvas in Paddy's account of the relationships and the community in which he lives.

# Study skills

## How to use quotations

One of the secrets of success in writing essays is the way you use quotations. There are five basic principles:
- Put inverted commas at the beginning and end of the quotation
- Write the quotation exactly as it appears in the original
- Do not use a quotation that repeats what you have just written
- Use the quotation so that it fits into your sentence
- Keep the quotation as short as possible

Quotations should be used to develop the line of thought in your essays.

Your comment should not duplicate what is in your quotation. For example:

> Paddy writes that he would rather stay in the circle with the gang than go with Liam: 'It was good being in the circle, better than where Liam was going.'

Far more effective is to write:

> Paddy reflects that 'It was good being in the circle, better than where Liam was going.'

However, the most sophisticated way of using the writer's words is to embed them into your sentence:

> Mr Clarke 'didn't look up' when Paddy wanted to show him the medal, and when he finally shakes his son's hand, Paddy 'wished he'd done it the first time'.

When you use quotations in this way, you are demonstrating the ability to use text as evidence to support your ideas – not simply including words from the original to prove you have read it.

Everyone writes differently. Work through the suggestions given here and adapt the advice to suit your own style and interests. This will improve your essay-writing skills and allow your personal voice to emerge.

The following points indicate in ascending order the skills of essay writing:

- Picking out one or two facts about the story and adding the odd detail
- Writing about the text by retelling the story
- Retelling the story and adding a quotation here and there
- Organising an answer which explains what is happening in the text and giving quotations to support what you write

........................................................................

- Writing in such a way as to show that you have thought about the intentions of the writer of the text and that you understand the techniques used
- Writing at some length, giving your viewpoint on the text and commenting by picking out details to support your views
- Looking at the text as a work of art, demonstrating clear critical judgement and explaining to the reader of your essay how the enjoyment of the text is assisted by literary devices, linguistic effects and psychological insights; showing how the text relates to the time when it was written

The dotted line above represents the division between lower- and higher-level grades. Higher-level performance begins when you start to consider your response as a reader of the text. The highest level is reached when you offer an enthusiastic personal response and show how this piece of literature is a product of its time.

*Coursework essay*

Set aside an hour or so at the start of your work to plan what you have to do.

- List all the points you feel are needed to cover the task. Collect page references of information and quotations that will support what you have to say. A helpful tool is the highlighter pen: this saves painstaking copying and enables you to target precisely what you want to use.
- Focus on what you consider to be the main points of the essay. Try to sum up your argument in a single sentence, which could be the closing sentence of your essay. Depending on the essay title, it could be a statement about a character: Kevin is the dominant member of the gang who the others are afraid to defy, and it is not until the end of the novel that Paddy, motivated by his anxiety over his home situation, dares to stand up to him; an opinion about the use of language: The realistic portrayal of a gang of ten-year-olds is enhanced by the way in which Paddy's narrative jumps abruptly from one subject to another sometimes totally unrelated one, in mid-sentence; or a judgement on a theme: The break-up of Mr and Mrs Clarke's marriage impinges on the reader's consciousness gradually, at first in vague hints, then in more obvious ways, just as it does in Paddy's ten-year-old mind.
- Make a short essay plan. Use the first paragraph to introduce the argument you wish to make. In the following paragraphs develop this argument with details, examples and other possible points of view. Sum up your argument in the last paragraph. Check you have answered the question.
- Write the essay, remembering all the time the central point you are making.
- On completion, go back over what you have written to eliminate careless errors and improve expression.

Read it aloud to yourself, or, if you are feeling more confident, to a relative or friend.

If you can, try to type your essay, using a word processor. This will allow you to correct and improve your writing without spoiling its appearance.

*Examination essay*

The essay written in an examination often carries more marks than the coursework essay even though it is written under considerable time pressure.

In the revision period build up notes on various aspects of the text you are using. Fortunately, in acquiring this set of York Notes on *Paddy Clarke Ha Ha Ha*, you have made a prudent beginning! York Notes are set out to give you vital information and help you to construct your personal overview of the text.

Make notes with appropriate quotations about the key issues of the set text. Go into the examination knowing your text and having a clear set of opinions about it.

In most English Literature examinations you can take in copies of your set books. This is an enormous advantage although it may lull you into a false sense of security. Beware! There is simply not enough time in an examination to read the book from scratch.

*In the examination*

- Read the question paper carefully and remind yourself what you have to do.
- Look at the questions on your set texts to select the one that most interests you and mentally work out the points you wish to stress.
- Remind yourself of the time available and how you are going to use it.
- Briefly map out a short plan in note form that will keep your writing on track and illustrate the key argument you want to make.
- Then set about writing it.
- When you have finished, check through to eliminate errors.

*To summarise, these are the keys to success:*

- **Know the text**
- **Have a clear understanding of and opinions on the storyline, characters, setting, themes and writer's concerns**
- **Select the right material**
- **Plan and write a clear response, continually bearing the question in mind**

# Sample essay plan

A typical essay question on *Paddy Clarke Ha Ha Ha* is followed by a sample essay plan in note form. This does not present the only answer to the question, merely one answer. Do not be afraid to include your own ideas and leave out some of the ones in this sample! Remember that quotations are essential to prove and illustrate the points you make.

**How successful is Roddy Doyle in getting inside the mind of a child in *Paddy Clarke Ha Ha Ha*?**

*Introduction*

Adventurous book in terms of language, structure and subject matter.

Unlike other autobiographical novels, it sustains the childish style of narration throughout.

Uses language, vocabulary, speech patterns, ideas and sentence structure of a child to convey the child's **viewpoint** (see Literary Terms) and omit that of the adult author.

*Part 1*

Narrative structure: chaotic, **episodic**, no chapter-divisions. Difficult to split one section from another except by looking at the hints about the marriage break-up.

Lots of **non sequiturs**, illogical interruptions, references to unrelated events in the middle of an incident or even in the middle of a sentence; jumps from one thing to another just as children do in conversation and sometimes in writing.

Only one real **flashback** (pp. 90–1), others are just jumbled memories. Novel breaks many structural rules in an attempt to convey the chaotic mind of a boy. Give examples (such as Grand National game, medical inspection) where Paddy's memories or researched facts interrupt the narrative.

Incessant questions are asked throughout the narrative, often of his parents, again typically reflecting the habit of a bright child (give some examples, such as the pages of dialogue surrounding the 'World War Three Looms Near' newspaper headline on pp. 22–6).

Sentence structure: often short simple sentences are used, rather as a child would speak or write, and when longer sentences are used their **syntax** often collapses into semi-nonsense.

*Part 2*        Vocabulary: on the whole, with some exceptions (give examples if you can, such as the rather literary description of the headmaster's study on p. 205) the vocabulary is simple, as a bright child of ten would use. Even some of the more **metaphorical** descriptions, (e.g. Mr O'Connell making a 'volcano' out of mashed potato for Liam and Aidan) recall typical childish fascinations. Words like 'brilliant' and 'sad' are used to describe most things.

Show how the vocabulary reflects the contradictions and ambiguous relationships of childhood (e.g. Liam and Aidan are Paddy's friends 'because we hated them').

Voracious reading enables Paddy to introduce unusual vocabulary which shows his fascination with words (give examples), but even then the new words which he learns are used in rude sentences about sex, snot or excrement by Paddy and his friends, reflecting young boys' typical obsessions.

*Part 3*     The content of the story reflects the interests, obsessions and preoccupations of a child of ten.

Football and Paddy's passion for Manchester United is an ongoing theme.

Give examples to explain how his admiration for heroes as varied as footballer George Best, Apache Indian Geronimo, television spy Napoleon Solo and Father Damien is revealed in detail.

*Part 4*     The humour of the novel lies in some of the feelings that young boys have (for example, about having a medical inspection, especially if a female nurse might touch certain parts of their anatomy), and in the mischief they get up to (e.g. raiding shops, writing their names in cement, lighting fires, etc.). It is a cruel humour, typical of children.

Younger brothers are physically tortured, and the **set pieces** like the swear word game are breathtakingly funny but also slightly sinister, as when Kevin whacks the others with the poker and Liam is declared an outcast for crying.

*Conclusions*   Summary and own opinions: all of these elements together are successful in **realistically** getting inside the mind of a child. Give your opinion on how well it is sustained; are we ever conscious of the author's presence or is it just Paddy's voice we hear? Is Paddy a 'real boy' or do you think the mischief is overdone?

Aim to present your personal view of the novel and the author's degree of success in convincing you that a child is telling the story.

Make a plan as shown above and attempt these questions:

1 Defend *Paddy Clarke Ha Ha Ha* against the accusation that it has nothing worthwhile to say.

2 Show how the break-up of the Clarkes' marriage gradually forces itself on Paddy and what effects it has on him.

3 Who or what are the main influences in Paddy's life? Write in detail about three of them.

4 Write a character study of two of the following: Mr Clarke, Mrs Clarke, Mr Hennessey. Show what effect each of the two has on Paddy.

5 The novel depicts vividly the way young boys operate in gangs. Write about the role of two of the following in the gang: Paddy, Kevin, Liam, Sinbad.

6 *Paddy Clarke Ha Ha Ha* is a very funny book but it is also incredibly sad. Write about what made you laugh in this book, and also about what made you feel sad.

7 Do you find Paddy Clarke a likeable character? Write about your reactions to him, supporting what you say by close reference to the novel.

8 It is quite hard to say what actually 'happens' in this novel. What is it that sustains your interest and makes you want to read on?

9 *Paddy Clarke Ha Ha Ha* won the Booker Prize when it was published in 1993. Why do you think the judges chose it?

10 Imagine that you are Mr Hennessey, the boys' teacher. How would you assess and describe Paddy, Kevin, Liam and Charles Leavy? If you wish you may try to write in his style.

11 *Paddy Clarke Ha Ha Ha* is about a childhood in 1960s Ireland. What aspects of the book are relevant to childhood and growing up in any time or place?

# PART FIVE

# CULTURAL CONNECTIONS

## BROADER PERSPECTIVES

*Paddy Clarke Ha Ha Ha* is unique in the way in which the author sustains the child's language and viewpoint (see Literary Terms), but other novels which deal with similar themes or ideas include the following.

### JAMES JOYCE: A PORTRAIT OF THE ARTIST AS A YOUNG MAN

This is an autobiographical novel about an Irish childhood, like *Paddy Clarke Ha Ha Ha*. James Joyce begins by presenting events using a young child's language and viewpoint (see Literary Terms), but later adapts the style and language as the hero, Stephen Dedalus, grows older. The viewpoint of the young man is sustained throughout, and Stephen's adventures at home and school make vivid and entertaining reading.

### BARRY HINES: A KESTREL FOR A KNAVE

The background is Barnsley rather than Ireland, but the portrayal of deprivation and the effect of marital breakdown on a boy are equally vivid. Billy lives on an inner-city estate and the novel explores the ways in which his family situation affects him. The only escape he seems to have from a downward spiral into petty crime is his relationship with Kes, his kestrel hawk. Like *Paddy Clarke Ha Ha Ha*, the book has its grim humour and bleaker moments.

### NIGEL HINTON: BUDDY

*Buddy* is a novel which deals with adolescence rather than boyhood, exploring the effect that family relationships and marital breakdown have on a teenage boy. Following his father's involvement in petty crime, Buddy's mother leaves home, and he has to grow up suddenly and learn to manage without her.

### WILLIAM GOLDING: LORD OF THE FLIES

Arguably the best novel about young boys as they really are, without the presence and control of adults. A group of schoolboys on their way to be evacuated from a nuclear war crash-land on a deserted Pacific island. All the adults are killed, rescue is uncertain and the boys must fend for themselves. At first they have a wonderful time living out every young boy's dream – no grown-ups; a perfect island paradise – but things begin to go wrong and the savage climax (see Literary Terms) approaches swiftly. *Paddy Clarke Ha Ha Ha* has some similar qualities, as William Golding observes vividly the inner lives of the gang when they are away from their parents.

# LITERARY TERMS

**atmosphere** a common term for the mood which dominates a piece of writing

**authorial comment** an intrusion in which the author comments on the events or characters described in the narrative. Such intrusions virtually never occur in *Paddy Clarke Ha Ha Ha*, as the viewpoint of the ten-year-old Paddy is sustained throughout; otherwise the narrative would seem less realistic, since we would be constantly reminded of the fact that the narrative is actually written by Roddy Doyle rather than Paddy Clarke

**autobiographical** an autobiography is the story of a person's life written by that person. A literary work such as a novel, poem or play, even though it is fiction, can be autobiographical if it conveys experiences and feelings drawn from the author's own life

*Bildungsroman* (German: 'formation-novel') a novel concerned with describing a central character's development from childhood to maturity

**character** an invented, imaginary person in a work of literature (though characters may be based on real people), with human qualities and behaviour

**climax** a moment of great intensity which is the culmination of a sequence of events in a narrative. Despite the lack of plot in *Paddy Clarke Ha Ha Ha*, the moments when Paddy becomes aware of the true situation regarding his parents are climactic, while the events towards the end of the novel come to a climax as his divorce from his friends parallels that at home

**colloquialism** the use of the kinds of expression and grammar associated with ordinary, everyday speech rather than formal language. This is one of the features of Paddy's narration which make it feel like that of a ten-year-old child

**dialect** a form of a language spoken in a particular area or locality (in *Paddy Clarke Ha Ha Ha*, the English spoken in Dublin), with specialist vocabulary typical of speech rather than of writing

**dialogue** the speech and conversation between characters in any literary work

**empathise** to mentally identify with a character in a story, to the point of fully understanding his or her thoughts, feelings and actions

**episodic** written in the form of a series of separable incidents

**flashback** a sudden jump backwards in time to an earlier episode or incident

**irony** a use of language in which a speaker or writer states one thing but means something else

**metaphor** a departure from literal writing in which one thing is described as being another, for example 'The barn became surrounded by skeleton houses' (p. 11): the houses are only partly built, and are 'skeletons' because Paddy can see their insides and basic structure like the bones of a person with no skin or flesh

**narrative** a story, tale or recital of a specific selection of events, so as to suggest some relationship between them

**narrator** the person who tells the story. The narrator can be distinguished from the author of a work, as in *Paddy Clarke Ha Ha Ha*, where we believe Paddy Clarke to be narrating the story although we know that Roddy Doyle is the author

**non sequitur** (Latin: 'it does not follow') an illogical deviation in thought or narrative, as when Paddy suddenly thinks of something totally unrelated to what he is describing and immediately inserts it into the next sentence or paragraph

**pathos** a strong feeling of pity or sorrow

**realism** telling things as they are, often in haphazard detail, evoking real and life-like experiences; many of Paddy's vivid narrations seem realistic

**set piece** a vivid, almost separate incident in a novel which universally evokes readers' experiences of this type of event. The Grand National game or the football match are examples of set pieces in *Paddy Clarke Ha Ha Ha*, as they evoke in many adult readers recollections of similar memorable events in their own childhoods

**structure** the overall principle of organisation in a work of literature

**style** the characteristic manner in which a writer expresses himself or herself, or the particular manner of an individual work

**symbol** an object or idea which is used to represent some other idea or quality

**syntax** the grammatical structure of sentences

**viewpoint** the perspective from which the events, characters and narrator in a literary work are seen. The viewpoint in *Paddy Clarke Ha Ha Ha* is solely that of the narrator Paddy, with the author's point of view rarely (if ever) intruding on the narrative

# TEST ANSWERS

**TEST YOURSELF (Section 1 pp. 1–66)**

**A** 1 Paddy *(p. 30)*
2 Mrs Clarke *(p. 3)*
3 Mr Hennessey *(p. 63)*
4 Mr Clarke *(p. 46)*
5 Liam and Aidan's house *(p. 29)*
6 Mrs Kiernan *(p. 53)*

**TEST YOURSELF (Section 2 pp. 67–134)**

**A** 1 Mrs Quigley *(p. 67)*
2 Sinbad *(p. 81)*
3 Laurence Hanley *(p. 71)*
4 Ian McEvoy *(p. 103)*
5 Alan Baxter's Scalextric set *(p. 99)*
6 Mr Clarke *(p. 110)*

**TEST YOURSELF (Section 3 pp. 134–84)**

**A** 1 Aidan *(p. 148)*
2 Cyril, the butcher *(p. 175)*
3 Mr O'Keefe *(p. 151)*
4 Mr Clarke *(p. 179)*
5 Mrs Clarke *(p. 142)*
6 Seán Whelan *(p. 161)*
7 Aidan *(p. 169)*

**TEST YOURSELF (Section 4 pp. 184–246)**

**A** 1 David Geraghty *(p. 245)*
2 Paddy *(p. 212)*
3 Charles Leavy *(p. 234)*
4 Mr Clarke *(p. 213)*
5 Kevin *(p. 237)*
6 Sinbad *(p. 185)*

## GCSE and equivalent levels (£3.50 each)

Maya Angelou
*I Know Why the Caged Bird Sings*

Jane Austen
*Pride and Prejudice*

Alan Ayckbourn
*Absent Friends*

Elizabeth Barrett Browning
*Selected Poems*

Robert Bolt
*A Man for All Seasons*

Harold Brighouse
*Hobson's Choice*

Charlotte Brontë
*Jane Eyre*

Emily Brontë
*Wuthering Heights*

Shelagh Delaney
*A Taste of Honey*

Charles Dickens
*David Copperfield*

Charles Dickens
*Great Expectations*

Charles Dickens
*Hard Times*

Charles Dickens
*Oliver Twist*

Roddy Doyle
*Paddy Clarke Ha Ha Ha*

George Eliot
*Silas Marner*

George Eliot
*The Mill on the Floss*

William Golding
*Lord of the Flies*

Oliver Goldsmith
*She Stoops To Conquer*

Willis Hall
*The Long and the Short and the Tall*

Thomas Hardy
*Far from the Madding Crowd*

Thomas Hardy
*The Mayor of Casterbridge*

Thomas Hardy
*Tess of the d'Urbervilles*

Thomas Hardy
*The Withered Arm and other Wessex Tales*

L.P. Hartley
*The Go-Between*

Seamus Heaney
*Selected Poems*

Susan Hill
*I'm the King of the Castle*

Barry Hines
*A Kestrel for a Knave*

Louise Lawrence
*Children of the Dust*

Harper Lee
*To Kill a Mockingbird*

Laurie Lee
*Cider with Rosie*

Arthur Miller
*The Crucible*

Arthur Miller
*A View from the Bridge*

Robert O'Brien
*Z for Zachariah*

Frank O'Connor
*My Oedipus Complex and other stories*

George Orwell
*Animal Farm*

J.B. Priestley
*An Inspector Calls*

Willy Russell
*Educating Rita*

Willy Russell
*Our Day Out*

J.D. Salinger
*The Catcher in the Rye*

William Shakespeare
*Henry IV Part 1*

William Shakespeare
*Henry V*

William Shakespeare
*Julius Caesar*

William Shakespeare
*Macbeth*

William Shakespeare
*The Merchant of Venice*

William Shakespeare
*A Midsummer Night's Dream*

William Shakespeare
*Much Ado About Nothing*

William Shakespeare
*Romeo and Juliet*

William Shakespeare
*The Tempest*

William Shakespeare
*Twelfth Night*

George Bernard Shaw
*Pygmalion*

Mary Shelley
*Frankenstein*

R.C. Sherriff
*Journey's End*

Rukshana Smith
*Salt on the snow*

John Steinbeck
*Of Mice and Men*

Robert Louis Stevenson
*Dr Jekyll and Mr Hyde*

Jonathan Swift
*Gulliver's Travels*

Robert Swindells
*Daz 4 Zoe*

Mildred D. Taylor
*Roll of Thunder, Hear My Cry*

Mark Twain
*Huckleberry Finn*

James Watson
*Talking in Whispers*

William Wordsworth
*Selected Poems*

*A Choice of Poets*

*Mystery Stories of the Nineteenth Century including The Signalman*

*Nineteenth Century Short Stories*

*Poetry of the First World War*

*Six Women Poets*